IN SEARCH OF TRUTH

A Step-by-Step Guide to
Security and Personal Fulfillment

**by
Derek Prince**

Sovereign World Ltd.,
P.O. Box 17,
Chichester PO20 6YB,
England

© Derek Prince
Derek Prince Ministries,
P.O. Box 300,
Fort Lauderdale,
Florida FL 33302,
U.S.A.

ISBN 1 85240 033 1

Printed and bound in Great Britain by
Richard Clay Ltd., Bungay, Suffolk

IN SEARCH OF TRUTH

Table of Contents

1. THE MASTER PLAN

The title of this book – *In Search of Truth* – has a very personal meaning for me. The book is, in fact, the outcome of my own search for the truth, which extended over many years.

For as long as I can remember, I had a deep, but unexplainable, conviction that there must be a meaning and a purpose to existence – something for which it would be worth living and even – if need be – dying. Although I became immersed in a succession of activities that had no bearing on this issue, I never lost this inner conviction. It was as much a part of me as my five senses.

I was educated in British boarding schools from the age of nine – first at a preparatory school in Kent and then, from age 13 to 18, as a scholar of Eton College. Throughout these years, attendance at the school chapel was obligatory. Outwardly I conformed, but inwardly I always knew there was something missing. Did these people really believe all the things they said so glibly in church? Certainly there was nothing there that could satisfy my quest.

From Eton I went on to King's College, Cambridge, as the senior scholar of my year. I had already concluded that religion did not have the answer to my quest, but I was not prepared to give up. Where else could I turn? The obvious answer seemed to be philosophy – the search for wisdom.

For the next seven years I studied philosophy in two main branches: Greek philosophy (especially that of Plato) and contemporary linguistic philosophy under the personal supervision of Ludwig Wittgenstein (who was recognized as the "father" of this philosophic school). For two years I was the senior research student of the University, and finally I was elected into a fellowship in King's College, Cambridge.

Yet, in spite of my academic success, I was still frustrated in my quest. I had been confronted with all sorts of different theories, but none of them seemed to explain the real purpose of existence. Where could I turn now?

At this point, however, the outbreak of World War II relieved me of the need to make any decision about my immediate future. I knew that I would shortly be called up into the British Army. I would thus be cut off from all the libraries and other learning resources to which I was accustomed. I was confronted with one urgent question: What should I take with me to read in the army?

To my own surprise, logic supplied a clear and practical answer: *the Bible*. Objectively, I recognized it as the most widely read and influential book in the history of the human race. Certainly, too, it dealt with the theme that was the object of my quest. Yet I had to acknowledge that I knew very little about it! I concluded that it was my intellectual duty to study the Bible – but as a work of philosophy, not of religion. Accordingly, I bought myself a new black Bible, containing the Old and New Testaments in the 1611 King James Version, and I took this with me into the army. (Somehow I could not imagine a Bible being any other color but black!)

Contrary to all my expectations, my next 5–1/2 years in the army were more fruitful than all my previous years at Eton and Cambridge. At first, however, my attempts to study the Bible proved intensely frustrating. I did not know where to begin or what to look for. I did not even know how to classify the Bible. Was it philosophy? Or religion? Or history? Or magnificent poetry? The Bible contained elements of all these, but none of them adequately described its totality.

It is not my purpose here to describe all the different phases of my search. Central to it were three years spent in the arid deserts of North Africa. Here I found myself in a kind of intellectual "vacuum" which accentuated my isolation from my familiar academic and cultural environment. There were no distractions to come between me and the Bible.

This sustained and concentrated exposure to the Bible gave me a new perspective on life, quite unlike the man–centered views which had prevailed in philosophy. A new system of concepts produced in me new patterns of thought. My whole picture of myself and the world around me changed radically.

I discovered that the Bible could be compared to a human body: a skeleton clothed with successive layers of muscle, flesh, skin, hair, etc. Like a medical student learning anatomy, I worked my way through the externals and down to the skeleton. Gradually there unfolded before me a master plan for the human race, perfect in every detail, extending from eternity to eternity.

Just as the human skeleton is built around the spine, I found that the plan unfolded in the Bible also had its "spine" – something that held the whole together and into which all the other parts were fitted. This "spine" of all biblical revelation is a *person*, described as Messiah and Redeemer. All the other parts of the Bible become clear and meaningful when seen in their relationship to this Messiah-Redeemer.

What excited me most was that the Bible also revealed certain practical steps by which I could enter personally into the master plan and find a place in it that was specially appointed for me. As I followed these steps – not without trepidation – I found that I had become part of the plan! I did not have to write my own scenario. It had already been written for me. Instead, I had to learn how to play my appointed role.

Entering into the plan brought me into a wonderful new relationship with the Messiah-Redeemer who is the "spine" of the skeleton. I learned something which went beyond all my previous speculations in the field of philosophy. I discovered that truth is not an abstraction. On the contrary, *truth is a person*. To discover truth in its fullness is to discover a person.

In the years that have elapsed since then, I have encountered many people – from many different backgrounds and cultures – who are motivated by the same quest that had motivated me. It has been my joy and privilege to direct them along the same path that I had followed. I am aware, however, that there are countless other such "seekers" whom I will never come to know personally. It is for the benefit of such people that I have prepared these studies.

My purpose in this book is to guide you in a systematic study of the Bible which will accomplish three results. First, it will lay bare the master plan which is the "skeleton" around which the whole Bible is built. Second, it will bring you face to face with the Messiah–Redeemer who is the "spine" into which all the other parts of the skeleton are fitted. Third, it will show you the practical steps which you must take to find your special place in the master plan.

The first key figure in the unfolding of the plan is a man who lived 4,000 years ago: Abraham. From him, there descended a nation that produced seers, prophets, artists, musicians and statesmen, all of whom made their special contributions to the plan's unfolding. Its full outworking, however, had to wait for the manifestation of the Messiah–Redeemer. Through Him the plan now embraces all lands and all peoples of the earth.

The studies in this book begin with Abraham and then follow in logical order the successive stages of the plan's unfolding.

Perhaps you may ask: "If I follow through these Studies, what result can I expect in my life? What will be my reward for all the work involved?" The answer can be given in one word: WISDOM. But it will not be the wisdom of traditional philosophy, which is subjective and speculative. The wisdom contained in the Bible is of a different order, proceeding from a different source. No better description of it can be given than that which is found in the writings of the world's wisest man, Solomon:

> *My son, if you receive my words,*
> *And treasure my commands within you,*
> *So that you incline your ear to wisdom,*
> *And apply your heart to understanding;*
> *Yes, if you cry out for discernment,*
> *And lift up your voice for understanding,*
> *If you seek her as silver,*
> *And search for her as for hidden treasures;*
> *Then you will understand the fear of the Lord,*
> *And find the knowledge of God.*   (Proverbs 2:1-5)

Solomon here outlines four conditions that the seeker after wisdom must fulfill:

First, *open-mindedness* – a willingness to lay aside prejudices and preconceptions, so as to receive and retain the truths revealed in the Bible.

Second, *humility* – an ear that is bowed down in reverence to hear what God has to say.

Third, *prayer* – a voice continually calling out to God in earnest petition for His guidance.

Fourth, *hard work* – compared to digging for treasure buried in the earth.

What, then, is the treasure that is promised to the faithful seeker? It is summed up in one phrase so simple and yet so profound that it passes human comprehension: *the knowledge of God*.

The eternal, omnipotent God revealing Himself in all His many-sided aspects and attributes to frail, confused humanity! Who could even begin to fathom the depths of such knowledge? Yet this is the prize promised to every seeker who fulfills the conditions.

Finally, in the next verse, Solomon reveals the source of such wisdom and knowledge:

> *For the LORD gives wisdom;*
> *From His mouth come knowledge and understanding.*   (Proverbs 2:6)

God Himself alone is the source of this wisdom, and the Bible is the only pathway to that source.

2. HOW TO USE THIS BOOK

One of my philosophy professors once said: "The key to finding truth is to ask the right questions." This is the key which is now being placed in your hands.

At the head of each of the nineteen studies that follow, you will find a brief introductory paragraph explaining the general theme of the study. After that, you will be confronted by a carefully arranged series of questions. You will also be directed to one or more passages in the Bible where you can find the answer to each question. It will be your task to determine what you feel to be the correct answer and to write it in the place provided.

On the next two pages following the questions you will find Correct Answers and Explanatory Notes. By reference to these you will be able to check your own answers and to clear up certain problems that may have arisen.

One distinctive feature of this method of study is that you never need to fear that someone else's conclusions will be arbitrarily imposed upon you. It will always be both your privilege and your responsibility to determine what you feel to be the best answer to each question. The Correct Answers and Explanatory Notes are offered merely as guidelines. But you are always free to disagree with them – provided you have a sound, scriptural basis for your disagreement.

SYSTEM OF BIBLE REFERENCES

The translation of the Bible used throughout these studies is the New King James Version. In most respects this remains close to the 1611 King James ("Authorized") Version with which millions of readers are already familiar. On the other hand, it replaces the archaic phrases and forms of the 1611 Version with language more easily understood by contemporary readers.

Before embarking on the studies, you must learn where to find each book in the Bible and to understand the system of abbreviating the names of the books which is used throughout. (See the "Key to Abbreviated Names of Bible Books" on page 8.) References to passages of Scripture are given as follows: first, the book; second, the chapter; third, the verse.

For example, Gen. 3:15 indicates the book of Genesis, chapter 3, verse 15. Again, 2 Chron. 23:11 indicates the Second book of Chronicles, chapter 23, verse 11. In books which have no chapters, the verse number immediately follows the book. For example, Ob. 10 indicates the book of Obadiah, verse 10.

STEPS TO FOLLOW

Always commence each study by reading carefully through the Introduction. Then go on to answer the questions, all of which will be related to the theme of the Introduction.

In the first study, "God's Purpose for Israel," there are twenty-eight questions. In parentheses after each question there are references to one or more passages of Scripture. The answer to each question is always to be found in the passages referred to in the parentheses after that question. Following after each question, there is a space, indicated by one or more dotted lines, in which you must write your answer to the question. The correct procedure for answering the questions is as follows:

(1) Read the question carefully.

(2) Find the Scripture passages referred to in parentheses and read through these passages carefully, until you find the answer to that question.

(3) In the space indicated by the dotted lines, write down in brief simple language the answer which you have found.

Sometimes the answer to one question must be divided up into two or more parts. In such cases, the spaces for each part of the answer are numbered (1).......... (2).......... (3).......... etc. and each part of the answer must be written in the correct numbered space.

By way of example, you will find below two questions from Study No. 1, with the correct answers written in, to show you how and where to write your answers:

1. How many people did God promise Abraham would be blessed through him? (Gen. 12:3)

All the families of the earth

13. Provided Israel fulfilled these demands, what three things did God promise they would be? (Ex. 19:5-6)
(1) A special treasure above all people

(2) A kingdom of priests
....

(3) A holy nation
....

When doing these questions for yourself, do not merely write down the answers given above. First, look up the Scripture passages and work out your own answers. Then check your answers with the ones given above to see if they are correct. Then carry on answering the rest of the questions in the same way until you have completed the whole study.

MEMORY WORK

An important feature of each study is an appropriate passage of Scripture for you to memorize. You may be tempted to pass over this. But don't do so! The Bible reveals that truth must not merely be apprehended by the intellect; it must also be stored up in the heart. Systematic memorization is one most effective way to do this.

Think of these memory verses as mental "anchors." One or two relatively small anchors may be used to hold a very large ship firmly in position. In the same way, a brief memory verse may "anchor" a complete and important passage of Scripture in your mind.

If you have difficulties with memorization or do not know how to begin, here is a simple, practical method to follow. Take a blank card and on one side neatly print the study number in the top left-hand corner, and then the Scripture reference in the middle, followed by the study title. Here is how your first card should look, for example:

```
┌─────────────────────────────────────────────┐
│                                             │
│   Study No. 1                               │
│                                             │
│              Exodus 19:5-6                   │
│                                             │
│          God's Purpose for Israel           │
│                                             │
│                                             │
└─────────────────────────────────────────────┘
```

Then on the other side of the card neatly write the Scripture passage itself:

```
┌─────────────────────────────────────────────┐
│  "'Now therefore, if you will indeed obey My voice and
│  keep My covenant, then you shall be a special
│  treasure to Me above all people; for all the earth is
│  Mine. And you shall be to Me a kingdom of priests
│  and a holy nation.' These are the words which you
│  shall speak to the children of Israel."
└─────────────────────────────────────────────┘
```

Carry your memory cards with you. Whenever you have a spare moment during the day, take the opportunity to review your memory verses. Regular review is the secret of successful memory work. In this way you will be able to say in the words of the psalmist:

Your word I have hidden in my heart,
That I might not sin against You.   (Psalm 119:11)

PROGRESS ASSESSMENT SECTIONS

In addition to the memory work, you will also find three sections for Progress Assessment. These are interspersed with the studies at carefully chosen intervals. Their purpose is twofold:

First, to *encourage* you by an overview of what you have accomplished in the preceding studies.

Second, to help you *consolidate* all that you have learned, so that it becomes a permanent part of your mental and spiritual equipment.

Each of these sections will close with some assignments for systematic review, and then with a number of "theme" questions related to the material you have been working through.

You will be invited to consider carefully how you would answer each of these questions, and then to select one question to which you will *write out* an answer in your own words.

Remember: review is an essential part of all successful learning. Do not hurry through this section. Take all the time you need to assimilate all it contains.

PROCEDURE FOR WORKING THROUGH THE COURSE

Write in your answer to every question in Study No. 1, and then – with your Bible closed – write out the memory work in the space provided at the end. Then turn over to the Correct Answers to this study. Check your own answers by reference to these Correct Answers. If in any case your answer does not agree with the corresponding Correct Answer, read through both the question and the relevant Scripture passage again until you understand clearly the reason for the Correct Answer.

On the page opposite the Correct Answers you will find Notes on these Answers which explain them more fully. Take time to read through these Notes, and to look up any further passages of Scripture referred to in them.

Finally, evaluate your own work by writing against them each answer that you have given the mark you feel you deserve for that answer. A simple standard of marking is given together with the Correct Answers. If an answer is valued at more than one mark, do not allow yourself the full mark unless your answer is as complete as the Correct Answer. Remember that the marks for the Memory work are important!

Add up your marks for Study No. 1 and check this total by reference to the three standards given at the bottom of the Correct Answer: 60% or over rates as "Fair"; 75% or over as "Good"; 90% or over as "Excellent."

When you have completed all that there is to do in connection with Study No. 1, turn over to Study No. 2, and work through this in the same way. Continue like this until you have completed the whole course, including the Progress Assessment sections. The methods for doing Study Nos. 17 and 19 are slightly different, but they are clearly explained at the head of each study.

Remember! You must NEVER turn over to the Correct Answers for any study until you have first written in your own answer to every question in that study – including the Memory Work!

When you have completed the last study, turn over to the page headed "Marks for the Course." Write in your marks for each study in the space provided, add them up, and evaluate your standard of achievement for the course as a whole. However, you will find that the final evaluation cannot be expressed merely in terms of "marks," but only in terms of enduring spiritual blessings and achievements which will have come to you through faithfully working through the complete course.

FINAL PERSONAL ADVICE

(1) Begin each study with prayer, asking God to guide you and give you understanding.

(2) Do not work too quickly. Do not try to accomplish the whole study at one sitting. Read through each passage of Scripture several times, until you are sure of its meaning. It will often be helpful to read several verses before or after the actual passage in order to grasp its full meaning.

(3) Write neatly and clearly. Do not make your answers longer than necessary. Use a well sharpened pencil or a ball point pen.

(4) Pay special attention to the Memory Work.

(5) Pray daily that God may help you to apply in your own life the truths that you are learning.

KEY TO ABBREVIATED NAMES OF BIBLE BOOKS

BOOKS OF THE OLD TESTAMENT

I. THE LAW

Genesis	– Gen.
Exodus	– Ex.
Leviticus	– Lev.
Numbers	– Num.
Deuteronomy	– Deut.

II. HISTORY

Joshua	– Josh.
Judges	– Jud.
Ruth	– Ruth
1 Samuel	– 1 Sam.
2 Samuel	– 2 Sam.
1 Kings	– 1 Kin.
2 Kings	– 2 Kin.
1 Chronicles	– 1 Chron.
2 Chronicles	– 2 Chron.
Ezra	– Ezra
Nehemiah	– Neh.
Esther	– Est.

III. POETICAL

Job	– Job
Psalms	– Ps.
Proverbs	– Prov.
Ecclesiastes	– Ecc.
Song of Solomon	– Song

IV. MAJOR PROPHETS

Isaiah	– Is.
Jeremiah	– Jer.
Lamentations	– Lam.
Ezekiel	– Ezek.
Daniel	– Dan.

V. MINOR PROPHETS

Hosea	– Hos.
Joel	– Joel
Amos	– Am.
Obadiah	– Ob.
Jonah	– Jon.
Micah	– Mic.
Nahum	– Nah.
Habakkuk	– Hab.
Zephaniah	– Zeph.
Haggai	– Hag.
Zechariah	– Zec.
Malachi	– Mal.

BOOKS OF THE NEW TESTAMENT

I. GOSPELS

Matthew	– Matt.
Mark	– Mark
Luke	– Luke
John	– John

II. HISTORY

The Acts of the Apostles	– Acts

III. PAULINE EPISTLES

Romans	– Rom.
1 Corinthians	– 1 Cor.
2 Corinthians	– 2 Cor.
Galatians	– Gal.
Ephesians	– Eph.
Philippians	– Phil.
Colossians	– Col.
1 Thessalonians	– 1 Thess.
2 Thessalonians	– 2 Thess.
1 Timothy	– 1 Tim.
2 Timothy	– 2 Tim.
Titus	– Tit.
Philemon	– Philem.
Hebrews	– Heb.

IV. GENERAL EPISTLES

James	– Jam.
1 Peter	– 1 Pet.
2 Peter	– 2 Pet.
1 John	– 1 John
2 John	– 2 John
3 John	– 3 John
Jude	– Jude

V. PROPHECY

Revelation	– Rev.

(Note that "John" stands for the Gospel of John, but "1 John" for the First Epistle of John, and so on.)

STUDY NO. 1

GOD'S PURPOSE FOR ISRAEL

Introduction:

About 1,900 B.C.E. God chose a man named Abram (later renamed Abraham) to become the father of a nation for whom He planned a special destiny. God made a covenant with Abraham in which He promised that through his descendants all nations would be blessed. God confirmed this covenant to Abraham's son, Isaac, and to his grandson Jacob (whose name He changed to Israel).

Four hundred thirty years later, through Moses, God made a further covenant with Jacob's descendants, the nation of Israel, in which He gave them a complete set of laws and a fuller picture of their destiny. Later, God sent prophets to Israel who predicted how their destiny would be worked out.

Memory Work: Ex. 19:5-6   Please check when memory card prepared ☐

A. GOD'S PURPOSE REVEALED TO ABRAHAM

1. How many people did God promise Abraham would be blessed through him? (Gen. 12:3)

2. On what basis did God accept Abraham as righteous? (Gen. 15:6)

3. To how many people did God promise to make Abraham a father? (Gen. 17:4-5)

4. With whom did God make an everlasting covenant? (Gen. 17:7)

5. What promise did God give to Abraham in this covenant? (Gen. 17:7)

6. Which two descendants of Abraham were later included by name in this covenant? (Ex. 6:3-4   Lev. 26:42)

7. What new name did God give to Jacob? (Gen. 35:10)

8. What two pictures did God use to show Abraham how numerous his descendants would be? (Gen. 22:17)

    (1).. (2)..
9. How many people did God promise Abraham would be blessed in his seed? (Gen. 22:18)

10. Why did God promise this to Abraham? (Gen. 22:18)

11. What did God require Abraham to do for his children and his household in order to receive what God had promised him? (Gen. 18:19)

B. GOD'S PURPOSE REVEALED TO MOSES

12. What were the first two demands that God made on Israel when they came to Mount Sinai? (Ex. 19:5)

    (1).. (2)..
13. Provided Israel fulfilled these demands, what three things did God promise they would be? (Ex. 19:5-6)

    (1)..

    (2)..

    (3)..
14. What else did God promise Israel on the same conditions? (Deut. 28:1)

15. State two ways this would affect the attitude of other peoples toward Israel. (Deut. 28:10)

    (1)..

    (2)..
16. What would be the result of Israel's keeping God's covenant? (Deut. 29:9)

C. GOD'S PURPOSE REVEALED IN THE PSALMS AND PROPHETS

17. What are two ways in which God's favor and blessing on Israel will affect the rest of the world? (Ps. 67:1–2)

    (1)..

    (2)..

18. God promises to put His Spirit upon His chosen servant. What will this servant do for the Gentiles? (Is. 42:1)

    ....

19. State two things which God will appoint this servant to be for Israel and for the Gentiles. (Is. 42:6)

    (1)..

    (2)..

20. What two things did God choose Israel to be for Himself? (Is. 43:10a)

    (1).. (2)..

21. Name three ways in which God desired Israel to respond to His revelation of Himself. (Is. 43:10b)

    (1).. (2).. (3)................................

The prophets give a picture of a future period when God's purposes for Israel will have been fulfilled. The following questions relate to this period.

22. For what two purposes will many peoples go up to the mountain of the Lord? (Is. 2:2-3)

    (1)..

    (2)..

23. What two things will go forth from Zion and Jerusalem? (Is. 2:3)

    (1).. (2)..

24. At a time when the peoples of the earth are in deep darkness, what will the Lord do for Zion? (Is. 60:2)

    ....

25. How will the other nations and their rulers respond? (Is. 60:3)

    ....

26. At the time when the land of Israel is restored and rebuilt, what two titles will be given to Jews? (Is. 61:4-6)

    (1).. (2)..

27. For what two purposes will many peoples and mighty nations come up to Jerusalem? (Zech. 8:22)

    (1).. (2)..

28. What will men from other nations say to a Jew? (Zech. 8:23)

    ....

Memory Work: Exodus 19:5-6

Write out these verses from memory.

....

....

....

....

....

DO NOT TURN THIS PAGE UNTIL YOU HAVE COMPLETED ALL ANSWERS IN THIS STUDY

STUDY NO. 1: GOD'S PURPOSE FOR ISRAEL

CORRECT ANSWERS AND MARKS

Question No.	Answers	Marks
1.	All the families of the earth	1
2.	He (Abraham) believed God (or believed in God)	1
3.	Many nations (also translated Gentiles)	1
4.	With Abraham and his descendants	1
5.	To be God to him and to his descendants	1
6.	Isaac and Jacob	1
7.	Israel	1
8.	(1) The stars of the heaven (2) The sand on the seashore	2
9.	All the nations of the earth	1
10.	Because Abraham obeyed God's voice	1
11.	To command them to keep the way of the Lord by doing righteousness and justice	2
12.	(1) To obey God's voice (2) To keep God's covenant	2
13.	(1) A special treasure to God above all people	1
	(2) A kingdom of priests (3) A holy nation	2
14.	To set them high above all the nations of the earth	1
15.	(1) They would see that they are called by the name of the Lord	1
	(2) They would be afraid of Israel	1
16.	They would prosper in all that they did	1
17.	(1) God's way will be known on earth	1
	(2) God's salvation will be known among all the nations	1
18.	He will bring forth justice to the Gentiles	1
19.	(1) A covenant to the people (Israel)	1
	(2) A light to the Gentiles	1
20.	(1) His witnesses (2) His servant	2
21.	(1) To know (2) To believe (3) To understand	3
22.	(1) That He may teach them His ways	1
	(2) That they may walk in His paths	1
23.	(1) The law (2) The word of the Lord	2
24.	He will arise over her and His glory will be seen upon her	2
25.	They will come to her light and to the brightness of her rising	2
26.	(1) The Priests of the Lord (2) The Servants of our God	2
27.	(1) To seek the Lord of hosts (2) To pray before the Lord	2
28.	"Let us go with you, for we have heard that God is with you."	2

Consult Bible for written Memory Work

If word perfect, 4 marks for each verse 8
(1 mark off for each mistake. If more than three mistakes
in either verse, no marks for that verse.)

TOTAL 54

60% – 32   75% – 41   90% – 49

STUDY NO. 1: GOD'S PURPOSE FOR ISRAEL

NOTES ON CORRECT ANSWERS

(The numbers in the lefthand margin correspond to the
numbers of the correct answers on the previous page.)

1. From the beginning, God's purpose included all nations on earth.

2. The basis of Abraham's relationship with God was his faith.

3. "Abram" means "exalted father"; "Abraham" means "father of a multitude." Right from the beginning, God's purpose went beyond Abraham's immediate descendants to include people from every nation.

4-5. A covenant is the most solemn commitment that God can make. Every permanent relationship with God must be based on a covenant. (See Psalm 50:5.)

6-7. God's covenant was confirmed first to Isaac (not Ishmael); then to Jacob (renamed Israel); then to the nation descended from Jacob and named Israel.

8-9. God emphasized that the number of people who were to be blessed through Abraham was greater than he could imagine or calculate.

10. Abraham's faith was expressed in his obedience – even when that meant sacrificing his son.

11. The way that Abraham instructed and disciplined his household sets God's standard for all fathers. It was the reason why God chose him.

12. The key to all God's blessings is to obey His voice. (Compare Ex. 15:26 Deut. 28:1-2.)

13. These three promises sum up God's purpose for Israel.

14-15. God intended Israel to be a leader and a pattern for all other nations.

16. See note on No. 12.

17. God intended that the blessings He would bestow on Israel would flow from them to all other nations.

18-19. Ultimately, God's purposes for Israel will be fulfilled through the chosen servant here described.

20. See notes on Nos. 14-15 and 18-19.

21. This threefold response is necessary for Israel to fulfill God's purpose.

22-23. God intends Jerusalem to be a center of spiritual teaching for all nations.

24-25. This age will close with a period of worldwide distress and darkness, in the midst of which God will reveal His glory first to Zion, and then through Zion to the nations and their rulers.

26. The restoration of Israel will fulfill God's original purpose, stated in Ex. 19:6.

27-28. See note on Nos. 22-23.

STUDY NO. 2

ISRAEL'S FAILURE AND GOD'S SALVATION

Introduction:

Through Moses, God made a covenant with Israel which had two opposite sides. If Israel would be faithful to the covenant, they would be blessed above all other nations. But if they were unfaithful, God would bring upon them a series of judgments of ever-increasing severity. In subsequent history, Israel proved unfaithful and all the judgments which God predicted came upon them.

However, God promised that in the latter days a redeemer would come to Zion, and that Israel would receive forgiveness and cleansing from all their sins and would become once more a holy nation.

Memory Work: Is. 43:25   Please check when memory card prepared ☐

(Review daily Ex. 19:5-6)

A. ISRAEL'S FAILURE

1. What did Moses warn Israel they would do after his death? (Deut. 31:29a)

....

....

2. Why would disaster come upon Israel in the latter days? (Deut. 31:29b)

....

....

3. Three times God warned Israel against acting in a certain way toward Him. What was that way? (Lev. 26:21, 23, 27)

....

4. If Israel refused God's warnings, a series of evil consequences would come upon them. State those described in the following verses of Lev. ch. 26:

    (1) v.25 (a).. (b)...

             (c).. (d)...

    (2) v.29...

    (3) v.31 (a).. (b)...

             (c)...

    (4) v.32 (a).. (b)...

    (5) v.33 (a).. (b)...

5. Of all the troubles listed in answers to questions 1 through 4 above, how many have actually come upon the Jewish people?

....

6. Daniel confessed various sins committed by his people. What are the ones he specifies in Dan. 9:5?

    (1).. (2)...

    (3).. (4)...

    (5)...

7. In what way had Israel disobeyed the voice of the Lord? (Dan. 9:10)

....

....

8. If Daniel were alive today, how many of the same sins would he need to confess on behalf of the Jewish people?

....

B. GOD'S SALVATION

9. God warned Israel that they would be driven out of their land but promised that He would not do two things to them. What were they? (Lev. 26:44)

    (1)...

    (2)...

....

10. What will God remember that will cause Him to show mercy to Israel? (Lev. 26:45)

....

....

11. For what does David pray to come out of Zion? (Ps. 14:7)

....

12. In the day when God's anger is turned away, what will Israel say concerning God's salvation? (Is. 12:2)

....

13. In what two forms does God reveal Himself to Israel? (Is. 43:3)

(1).. (2)..

14. Is there any other Savior? (Is. 43:11)

....

15. What does God promise concerning Israel's transgressions? (Is. 43:25)

....

16. What does God promise concerning Israel's sins? (Is. 43:25)

....

17. To whom in Zion does God promise a Redeemer? (Is. 59:20)

....

18. What will come to Zion? (Is. 62:11)

....

19. What will be with him? (Is. 62:11)

....

20. What will be before him? (Is. 62:11)

....

21. In the day when God restores Israel, in what two ways will He deal with their iniquities? (Jer. 33:7-8)

(1).. (2)..

22. In the day when God brings Israel back to their own land, how will He reveal Himself through them to the nations? (Ezek. 39:27)

....

Memory Work: Isaiah 43:25

Write out this verse from memory.

....

....

....

DO NOT TURN THIS PAGE UNTIL YOU HAVE COMPLETED ALL ANSWERS IN THIS STUDY.

STUDY NO. 2: ISRAEL'S FAILURE AND GOD'S SALVATION
CORRECT ANSWERS AND MARKS

Question No.	Answers	Marks
1.	Become utterly corrupt and turn from the way Moses commanded them	2
2.	Because they would do evil in the sight of the Lord, provoking Him to anger with the work of their hands	2
3.	Walking contrary to God	1
4.	(1) (a) War (a sword) against them	1
	(b) Gathered (= besieged) in their cities	1
	(c) Struck with pestilence (d) Delivered into enemies' hands	2
	(2) Eat their own children during the siege	1
	(3) (a) Cities laid waste (b) Sanctuaries destroyed	2
	(c) No more offerings to the Lord	1
	(4) (a) Land left desolate	1
	(b) Enemies dwell in, and be astonished at it	1
	(5) (a) Scattered among the nations (b) Pursued by the sword	2
5.	All	1
6.	(1) We have sinned (2) We have committed iniquity	2
	(3) We have acted wickedly (4) We have rebelled	2
	(5) We have departed from God's precepts and judgments	1
7.	They had not walked in His laws which He set before them by His prophets	2
8.	All	1
9.	(1) Not cast them away	1
	(2) Not abhor them so as to destroy them and break His covenant with them	2
10.	The covenant of their ancestors whom He brought out of the land of Egypt	2
11.	The salvation of Israel	1
12.	"God is/has become my salvation."	1
13.	(1) Their Holy One (2) Their Savior	2
14.	No	1
15.	He will blot them out	1
16.	He will not remember them	1
17.	To those who turn from transgression in Jacob	1
18.	Salvation	1
19.	His reward	1
20.	His work (recompense)	1
21.	(1) He will cleanse them (2) He will pardon them	2
22.	He will be hallowed in them	1

Consult Bible for written Memory Work
If word perfect, 4 marks — 4
(1 mark off for each mistake. If more than 3 mistakes, no marks)

TOTAL 49

60% – 29   75% – 37   90% – 44

STUDY NO. 2: ISRAEL'S FAILURE AND GOD'S SALVATION

NOTES ON CORRECT ANSWERS

(The numbers in the lefthand margin correspond to the
numbers of the correct answers on the previous page.)

1-2. Even before God gave Israel the covenant, He knew that they would break it. He had also prepared a way by which they could receive forgiveness and restoration.

3. The root of Israel's wrong *acts* was a wrong *attitude*: walking contrary to God. Another translation says, "act with hostility toward God."

4-5. The exact way in which these evil consequences came upon Israel is recorded partly in the Bible and partly in the writings of Josephus. They have continued also in later history.

6-8. The sins confessed by Daniel can be summed up in one word: rebellion.

9. God warned Israel that He would punish all their misdeeds, but He also promised that He would never finally reject them as His people. (Compare Jer. 33:23-26.)

10. Even though God's people may be unfaithful, God remains faithful to His covenant. (Compare Ps. 89:34.)

11-14. God's remedy for Israel's failure is summed up in one word: salvation. Only God Himself can be a Savior without compromising His own holiness.

15-16. God's salvation is so complete that He blots out our sins, so that He no longer remembers them.

17. God in His mercy offers Israel a redeemer, but Israel must respond by turning from their transgressions.

18-20. This redeemer brings three things with him: salvation, a reward, and a recompense.

21. Salvation includes both cleansing and pardon.

22. From the beginning, God's purpose has been to make Israel a blessing to the other nations and to reveal His holiness through Israel.

STUDY NO. 3

PORTRAIT OF MESSIAH (Part 1)

Introduction:

God foresaw that Israel would turn aside into sin and so fail to fulfill His purpose for them. In His mercy, however, He promised to send them a redeemer from the seed of David. Like David, this redeemer would be anointed with God's Holy Spirit and for this reason would be known as "Messiah" ("Anointed One"). In the New Testament, "Christ" means exactly the same as "Messiah." The coming of this Messiah is a central theme of the Old Testament (Hebrew: *Tenach*). The prophets describe very exactly how he would come and what he would do.

In the first century, Jewish writers who believed these promises described a man who fulfilled them and whom they acknowledged as Messiah. Their writings were collected in a book titled the New Testament (or Covenant). The questions in this study refer partly to the Old Testament and partly to the New Testament.

Memory Work: Mal. 3:1   Please check when memory card prepared ☐

(Review daily Is. 43:25)

A. MESSIAH'S GENEALOGY

1. To whom did God promise a special seed? (Gen. 22:15–18)

2. What did God promise to all nations through this seed? (Gen. 22:18)

3. Was Jesus descended from this ancestor? (Matt. 1:1)

4. What is now offered through Jesus to the Gentiles? (Gal. 3:13-14)

5. Through which of Abraham's two sons was the promised seed to come? (Gen. 17:19, 21)

6. Was Jesus descended from Isaac? (Matt. 1:2)

7. To which of his sons did Isaac transmit the blessing of Abraham? (Gen. 28:1-4)

8. Was this blessing extended also to this son's descendants? (Gen 28:4)

9. Was Jesus descended from Jacob? (Luke 3:34)

10. From which tribe of Israel was the ruler (Messiah) to come? (Gen. 49:10)

11. From which tribe did Jesus come? (Luke 3:33)

12. From which king of Israel was Messiah to be descended? (Ps. 89: 35-36 Is. 9:6-7)

13. Was Jesus descended from this king? (Matt. 1:6)

B. MESSIAH'S BIRTH

14. Where was Messiah to be born? (Micah 5:2)

15. Where was Jesus born? (Matt. 2:1 Luke 2:4-7)

16. What was to be unique about the birth of Messiah? (Is. 7:14)

17. What was unique about the birth of Jesus? (Matt. 1:18, 22-23 Luke 1:26-35)

18. Did Daniel provide a way to calculate when Messiah would come? (Dan. 9:25-26)

19. How many years after the decree to rebuild Jerusalem was Messiah to come? (Dan. 9:25)

20. Did Jesus come at the time predicted by Daniel?

C. MESSIAH'S MINISTRY

21. Was any messenger to precede the Messiah? (Mal. 3:1)

22. What was to be the task of this messenger? (Mal. 3:1)

23. Which messenger preceded Jesus? (Matt. 3:1-3; 11:7-10)

24. What was the task of this messenger? (Matt. 3:1-3; 11:7-10   Luke 1:76)

25. Of what was the Lord to come as a messenger? (Mal. 3:1)

26. Did God promise a new covenant to Israel? (Jer. 31:31-34)

27. Does that covenant provide for complete forgiveness of sins? (Jer. 31:34)

28. Did Jesus come to mediate such a covenant? (Heb. 9:13-15)

29. What did John the Baptist see descending upon Jesus in the form of a dove? (John 1:29-33)

30. Isaiah depicts a man anointed by the Holy Spirit (Is. 61:1). State four things this anointing would enable him to do.
   (1).. (2)..
   (3).. (4)..

31. After reading these words in the synagogue, what did Jesus say about Himself? (Luke 4:16-21)

32. With what did God anoint Jesus of Nazareth? (Acts 10:38)

33. State two things which this anointing enabled Jesus to do. (Acts 10:38)
   (1)..
   (2)..

34. Isaiah predicted that God would come to save Israel and would bring healing of four types of sickness. (Is. 35:4-6) List these four types.
   (1).. (2)..
   (3).. (4)..

35. List four types of sickness which Jesus healed. (Mark 8:22-25; 7:32-37   John 5:5-9   Matt. 9:32-33)
   (1).. (2)..
   (3).. (4)..

36. Upon what animal was Messiah to ride into Jerusalem? (Zech. 9:9)

37. Upon what animal (or animals) did the disciples place Jesus for His triumphal entry into Jerusalem? (Matt. 21:6-11   Mark 11:1-11)

Memory Work: Malachi 3:1
Write out this verse from memory.

STUDY NO. 3: PORTRAIT OF MESSIAH (Part 1)
CORRECT ANSWERS AND MARKS

Question No.	Answers	Marks
1.	To Abraham	1
2.	Blessing	1
3.	Yes	1
4.	The blessing of Abraham	1
5.	Isaac	1
6.	Yes	1
7.	Jacob	1
8.	Yes	1
9.	Yes	1
10.	Judah	1
11.	Judah	1
12.	David	1
13.	Yes	1
14.	Bethlehem of Judah	1
15.	Bethlehem of Judah	1
16.	He was to be born of a virgin	1
17.	He was born of a virgin	1
18.	Yes	1
19.	69 weeks, or a total of 483 Jewish years	1
20.	Yes	1
21.	Yes	1
22.	To prepare the way before Messiah	1
23.	John the Baptist	1
24.	To prepare the way before Jesus	1
25.	The covenant	1
26.	Yes	1
27.	Yes	1
28.	Yes	1
29.	The Holy Spirit	1
30.	(1) To preach good tidings to the poor	1
	(2) To heal the brokenhearted	1
	(3) To proclaim liberty to the captives	1
	(4) And opening of the prison to those who are bound	1
31.	"Today this Scripture is fulfilled in your hearing."	1
32.	With the Holy Spirit and with power	1
33.	(1) To go about doing good	1
	(2) To heal all who were oppressed by the devil	1
34.	(1) Blindness (2) Deafness (3) Lameness (4) Dumbness (Muteness)	4
35.	(1) Blindness (2) Deafness (3) Lameness (4) Dumbness (Muteness)	4
36.	On a donkey, a colt, the foal of a donkey	1
37.	On a donkey, a colt, the foal of a donkey	1

Consult Bible for written Memory Work. If word perfect, 4 marks ... 4

(1 mark off for each mistake. If more than 3 mistakes, no marks) TOTAL 51

60% – 31   75% – 38   90% – 46

STUDY NO. 3: PORTRAIT OF MESSIAH (Part 1)

NOTES ON CORRECT ANSWERS

(The numbers in the lefthand margin correspond to the
numbers of the correct answers on the previous page.)

1-6. God promised Abraham that through Isaac He would give him a posterity through whom blessing would come to all nations. Jesus the Messiah, descended from Abraham through Isaac, was the seed through whom the promise of blessing to all nations was fulfilled. (See Gal. 3:16.)

7-9. The promise of the "seed" through whom blessing was to come was passed down through Jacob. Thus, Messiah had to come from the line of the Jewish people.

10-13. God ordained that the ruler of Israel should come from the tribe of Judah. This was fulfilled first in David and then in Jesus, who was descended from David.

1-13. No one challenged the genealogy or the Davidic ancestry of Jesus while He was on earth. All Israel's genealogical records perished when the Second Temple was destroyed in 70 C.E. It is therefore impossible for anyone born after that date to prove His claim to be Messiah.

In Luke's genealogy of Jesus, he says only that Jesus was "supposed to be" the son of Joseph (Luke 3:23).

14-15. At the time of the birth of Jesus, the Jewish religious leaders were expecting the Messiah to be born in Bethlehem of Judah (see Matt. 2:1-6).

16-17. Note the following reasons for translating *almah* in this passage as "virgin": (1) The Jewish writers of the Septuagint translated it by *parthenos,* the standard Greek work for "virgin"; (2) No prophecy of the Tenach refers to a human father of Messiah, only to a mother (see Is. 49:1, 5   Ps. 22:9); (3) *Almah* describes a young woman, not yet married, which applied exactly to Mary; (4) In the Tenach *almah* is used only to refer to a virgin (see Gen. 24:43   Ex. 2:8); (5) The alternative Hebrew word *bethulah* in Joel 1:8 refers to a woman who has had a husband. Moreover, *bethulah* is sometimes used to personify a nation (see Is. 23:12; 47:1   Jer. 18:13; 31:4, 21).

18-20. According to Dan. 9:25-26, Messiah would come and then be cut off after 69 weeks (literally, "sevens") of years. Since the Jewish year is equivalent to 360 days, the actual number according to the Western calendar would be about 477 years. The decree to restore Jerusalem in the reign of Artaxerxes King of Persia was probably issued about 445 B.C.E. This would give a date of about 32 C.E. for the coming of Messiah the Prince. Jesus made His triumphal entry into Jerusalem about that time and shortly afterwards was "cut off." "The people of the prince that shall come" were the Roman legions under Titus who destroyed Jerusalem in 70 C.E.

25-28. The new covenant promised in Jer. 31:31-34 has three main features: (1) a new inner nature ("I will put My law in their minds, and write it on their hearts"); (2) a personal relationship with God ("they . . . shall know Me"); (3) forgiveness of sins ("I will forgive their iniquity, and their sin I will remember no more"). These features are all included in the covenant which Jesus instituted. Also, in Ezek. 16:59-60 God charges Israel with breaking the first covenant, but promises to replace it with an everlasting covenant.

29-35. The Holy Spirit coming down upon Jesus marked Him out as the promised Messiah. This equipped Him to be the deliverer of God's people from both sin and sickness.

34-35. The healing miracles of Jesus confirmed His identity as Messiah.

36-37. It was customary for a king to ride upon a donkey (see 2 Samuel 16:2).

STUDY NO. 4

PORTRAIT OF MESSIAH (Part 2)

Introduction:
The apostle Peter wrote concerning the prophets of the Old Testament that the Spirit of Messiah within them predicted the sufferings of Messiah and the glory that was to follow (1 Pet. 1: 10-11). At times these prophets spoke in the first person of going through experiences which never actually happened to them, but which did happen later in the life of Jesus. They described first the sufferings of Messiah and then the eternal glory into which He was to enter. Such predictions occur most frequently in the Psalms of David and in Isaiah. This study contains various examples.

Memory Work: Is. 53:4-5   Please check when memory card prepared ☐
(Review daily Mal. 3:1)

D. MESSIAH'S SUFFERING

38. Was Messiah to be accepted or rejected by His own people? (Is. 53:1-3)

39. Did Israel as a nation accept or reject Jesus? (John 1:11; 12:37-38)

40. By what kind of person was Messiah to be betrayed? (Ps. 41:9)

41. By whom was Jesus betrayed? (Mark 14:10)

42. Was this man a friend of Jesus? (Matt. 26:47, 50)

43. For what price was Messiah to be betrayed? (Zech. 11:12)

44. How much money did Jesus' betrayer receive? (Matt. 26:15)

45. What was to be done with the money of Messiah's betrayal? (Zech. 11:13)

46. What was done with the money of Jesus' betrayal? (Matt. 27:3-7)

47. Was Messiah to defend Himself before His accusers? (Is. 53:7)

48. How did Jesus react to His accusers? (Matt. 26:62-63; 27:12-14)

49. Was Messiah to be beaten and spat upon? (Is. 50:6)

50. Name two ways in which Jesus suffered at the hands of His oppressors. (Mark 14:65   John 19:1)

51. What kind of people were to be executed together with Messiah? (Is. 53:12)

52. Who were crucified together with Jesus? (Matt. 27:38)

53. Name two parts of Messiah's body that were to be pierced. (Ps. 22:16   Zech. 12:10)

54. Was Jesus pierced in His hands and feet? (Luke 24:39-40   John 20:25-27)

55. What was to happen to Messiah's garments and clothing? (Ps. 22:18)

56. What did the Roman soldiers do with the garments and tunic of Jesus? (John 19:23-24)

57. What would they give Messiah to drink? (Ps. 69:21)

58. What did they give Jesus to drink? (John 19:29)

59. What could not happen to Messiah's bones? (Ps. 34:19-20)

60. Were the bones of Jesus broken? (John 19:33,36)

61. What was the Lord to lay upon Messiah? (Is. 53:6)

62. What was to happen to Messiah as a result? (Is. 53:8)

63. What did Jesus bear on the cross? (1 Pet. 2:24)

64. What happened to Jesus as a result? (1 Pet. 3:18)

65. In the tomb of what kind of person was Messiah to be buried? (Is. 53:9)

66. In whose tomb was Jesus buried? (Matt. 27:57-60)

67. What kind of person was he? (Matt. 27:57)

E. MESSIAH'S VICTORY OVER DEATH

68. After Messiah's soul had become a sin offering, what three things are promised concerning Him?(Is. 53:10)

   (1)

   (2)

   (3)

69. Could these promises have been fulfilled if Messiah had remained dead?

70. What two things does God promise to His Holy One? (Ps. 16:10)

   (1)

   (2)

71. Were these two things fulfilled in the experience of David? (1 Kings 2:10   Acts 2:29)

72. In whose experience were they fulfilled? (Acts 2:30–32)

73. What position of authority did God promise to Messiah? (Ps. 110:1)

74. Could this have been fulfilled as long as He remained on earth?

75. To what place of authority did God exalt Jesus? (Acts 2:33-36)

76. Until what time must Jesus remain in heaven? (Acts 3:19-21)

77. How will Messiah come to establish His kingdom? (Dan. 7:13)

78. How will Jesus return from heaven? (Matt. 26:63-64)

79. On what mountain will Messiah's feet rest? (Zech. 14:4-5)

80. To what mountain will Jesus return? (Acts 1:9-12)

Memory Work: Isaiah 53:4-5
Write out these verses from memory.

DO NOT TURN THIS PAGE UNTIL YOU HAVE COMPLETED ALL ANSWERS IN THIS STUDY

STUDY NO. 4: PORTRAIT OF MESSIAH (Part 2)
CORRECT ANSWERS AND MARKS

Question No.	Answers	Marks
38.	He was to be rejected	1
39.	They rejected Him	1
40.	A close friend	1
41.	Judas Iscariot	1
42.	Yes	1
43.	Thirty pieces of silver	1
44.	Thirty pieces of silver	1
45.	It was to be cast to the potter in the house of the Lord	2
46.	It was cast down in the Temple and used to buy a potter's field	2
47.	No	1
48.	He remained silent	1
49.	Yes	1
50.	He was beaten and spat upon	2
51.	Transgressors	1
52.	Two robbers (transgressors)	1
53.	His hands and His feet	2
54.	Yes	1
55.	They were to divide His garments and cast lots for His clothing	2
56.	They divided His garments and cast lots for His clothing	2
57.	Vinegar	1
58.	Sour wine (i.e. vinegar)	1
59.	They could not be broken	1
60.	No	1
61.	The iniquity of us all	1
62.	He was to be cut off from the land of the living	2
63.	Our sins	1
64.	He was put to death	1
65.	A rich man	1
66.	Joseph of Arimathea	1
67.	A rich man	1
68.	(1) He shall see His seed (2) He shall prolong His days	2
	(3) The pleasure of the Lord shall prosper in His hand	1
69.	No	1
70.	(1) He will not leave His soul in Sheol	1
	(2) He will not allow Him to see corruption	1
71.	No	1
72.	The experience of Jesus	1
73.	To sit at God's right hand	1
74.	No	1
75.	God's right hand	1
76.	The times of restoration of all things	1
77.	With clouds of heaven	1
78.	With clouds of heaven	1
79.	The Mount of Olives	1
80.	The Mount of Olives	1

Consult Bible for written Memory Work

If word perfect, 4 marks for each verse 8
(1 mark off for each mistake. If more than 3 mistakes
in either verse, no marks for that verse)   TOTAL 61

60% – 37   75% – 46   90% – 55

STUDY NO. 4: PORTRAIT OF MESSIAH (Part 2)

NOTES ON CORRECT ANSWERS

(The numbers in the lefthand margin correspond to the
numbers of the correct answers on the previous page.)

38,47, Isaiah 52:13-53:12 is one of the great Messianic prophecies of the Old Testament.
51,61, It depicts a Servant of the Lord who is rejected by His own people, though without
62,65, any sin on His part, and who suffers the penalty of death for their iniquities. The
68. Jewish commentators have attempted to identify the "servant" of this passage as the
Jewish people, who have suffered at the hands of other nations. But this interpretation
cannot be valid for the following reasons:
(1) The "servant" here depicted was not guilty of any violence or deceit (see verse 9). This
does not apply to the Jewish people.
(2) The "servant" was wounded for the transgressions of others (see verses 4-6). Israel's
sufferings were caused by her own sins, as Moses had warned (see Lev. 26:14-43).
(3) By a personal knowledge of this servant, who bore the iniquities of others upon
Himself, many would be made righteous before God. This only comes through personal
faith in the Messiah (see Rom. 3:21-24).

39. Israel as a nation rejected Jesus. Nevertheless, there was a remnant who followed Him.
The early assembly of believers consisted mainly of Messianic Jews.

59-60. The Passover lamb, by whose blood the children of Israel were protected from the angel
of death, could not have any of its bones broken (Ex. 12:46). Jesus, as the sacrificial lamb
of God, likewise could not have any bones broken (John 1:29   1 Cor. 5:7).

61-64. The sacrifice of Jesus was foreshadowed each Day of Atonement when the high priest
transferred Israel's sins to the scapegoat (Lev. 16:21-22). Only the blood of the sacrifice
could atone for sin (Lev. 17:11). Therefore Jesus not only bore the sins of the people, but
also shed His blood for a full and final atonement (Heb. 9:13-22).

68-72. The resurrection of Jesus from the dead was God's vindication of Him as Messiah and
Lord (Rom. 1:3-4).

73-75. Jesus not only rose from the dead, but also ascended up to God the Father in heaven.
The right hand of God represents the seat of all authority and power in the universe.
Jesus has taken His place there, ruling in the midst of His enemies until all things
submit to His dominion (Ps. 110:2).

76. God has promised a period of restoration at the close of this age. This will center in the
restoration of Israel and will climax with the return of Messiah in glory (see Ps. 102:16).

77-80. The prophecies of Messiah's return in glory are even more numerous than those of His
first coming in humility.

STUDY NO. 5

A PROPHET LIKE MOSES

Introduction:
In Deuteronomy 18:18-19 Moses brings to Israel the following promise of God:

> *"I will raise up for them a Prophet like you from among their brethren, and will put My words in His mouth, and He shall speak to them all that I command Him.*
> *And it shall be that whoever will not hear My words, which He speaks in My name, I will require it of him."*

These words of Moses clearly establish three facts:

First, Moses here describes one particular prophet, whom God promises to send to Israel at a later time. The language that Moses uses is singular throughout: "a prophet" – "His mouth" – "He shall speak." These words cannot describe the later prophets in Israel as a whole. They must refer to one special prophet.

Second, this special prophet was to have unique authority, above all others who had gone before him. If anyone in Israel refused to hear this prophet, God would bring judgment upon that person.

Third, this prophet was to be like Moses in ways that would distinguish him from all other prophets who would ever come to Israel.

In Acts 3:22-26 the apostle Peter quotes these words of Moses and applies them directly to Jesus of Nazareth. A careful comparison of the Old and New Testaments shows over twenty distinct points of resemblance between Moses and Jesus. The following questions regarding the similarities between these two prophets are grouped according to three main headings: Childhood, Personal Experience and Ministry.

Memory Work: Deut. 18:18   Please check when memory card prepared ☐
(Review daily Is. 53:4-5)

A. THEIR CHILDHOOD

1. Name the Gentile emperor who imposed his rule on Israel at the time of the birth of each of these prophets. (Ex. 1:8-14   Luke 2:1-7)
   (1) Moses......................
   (2) Jesus......................
2. How were the lives of both Moses and Jesus endangered in their infancy? (Ex. 1:15-16   Matt. 2:16)

3. By whom were their lives saved? (Ex. 2:1-5   Heb. 11:23   Matt. 2:13-14)

4. With what people did each find refuge for a time? (Ex. 2:10   Matt. 2:14-15)

5. What intellectual ability did each display? (Acts 7:22   Luke 2:46-47   Matt. 13:54)

B. THEIR PERSONAL EXPERIENCES

6. Name two character traits common to each man. (Num. 12:3, 7   Matt. 11:29   Heb. 3:1-6)
   (1)... (2)........................
7. Were these prophets always received by Israel? (Ex. 2:14; 32:1   Num. 16:41   John 7:52   Matt. 27:21-22)

8. How did their brothers and sisters react to them at times? (Num. 12:1   Mark 3:21   Matt. 13:54-57   John 7:3-5)

9. How did each prophet respond before God in regard to the sin of Israel? (Ex. 32:31-32   Luke 23:34)

10. What was each willing to do to placate God's wrath against the sin of the people? (Ex. 32:31-32   Luke 23:34)

11. What did each of these prophets do at a crucial point in their lives? (Ex. 34:28   Matt 4:2)

12. Did each of these prophets enjoy special intimacy with God? (Num. 12:7-8   John 1:18 Matt. 11:27)

13. To what kind of place did each of these prophets go to have communion with God? (Ex. 24:12   Matt. 17:1, 5)

14. Did they take any disciples with them? (Ex. 24:13   Matt. 17:1)

15. What effect did that experience have on their physical bodies? (Ex. 34:29-30   Matt 17:2)

16. In what special way did God speak to them on at least one occasion? (Ex. 19:19-20 John 12:28-30)

17. Which supernatural beings guarded the burial place of each prophet? (Jude 9 Matt. 28:2-7)

C. THEIR MINISTRY

18. Name two other ministries, besides that of prophet, which each man exercised. (1) Deut. 4:1, 5   Matt. 5:1-2   John 3:1-2 (2)   Ps. 77:20   Is. 63:11   John 10:11, 14, 17) (1).. (2)..

19. What special, important truth about God did each reveal to God's people? (Ex. 3:13-15 John 17:6, 11)

20. What type of food did God supernaturally provide to His people through each of these prophets? (Ex. 16:14-15   Ps. 78:24   John 6:32-33, 51)

21. From what kind of slavery did Moses deliver Israel? (Ex. 3:10   Deut. 6:21)

22. From what kind of slavery did Jesus deliver those who believed in Him? (John 8:31-36)

23. How did both these prophets help the sick? (Ex. 15:25-26   Num. 21:6-9   Matt. 4:23; 8:16-17)

24. Was there any other prophet who worked such great miracles as these? (Deut. 34:10-12 John 5:36; 15:24   Acts 2:22)

25. What did each establish between God and His people? (Ex. 24:7-8   Matt. 26:26-28)

26. By what was it sealed? (Heb. 9:11-22)

Memory Work: Deuteronomy 18:18
Write out this verse from memory.

DO NOT TURN THIS PAGE UNTIL YOU HAVE COMPLETED ALL ANSWERS IN THIS STUDY

STUDY NO. 5: A PROPHET LIKE MOSES

CORRECT ANSWERS AND MARKS

Question No.	Answers	Marks
1.	(1) Pharaoh (2) Caesar Augustus	2
2.	Evil kings made decrees for each of them to be killed	1
3.	By the action of their parents	1
4.	The people of Egypt	1
5.	Unusual wisdom and understanding	1
6.	(1) Humility (2) Faithfulness to God	2
7.	No	1
8.	They criticized/rejected them	1
9.	Each prayed to God to forgive the people	1
10.	Each was willing to bear the punishment of the people	1
11.	Each fasted forty days	1
12.	Yes	1
13.	A high mountain	1
14.	Yes	1
15.	Their faces shone	1
16.	God spoke in an audible voice from heaven	1
17.	Angels	1
18.	(1) Teacher (2) Shepherd	2
19.	God's name	1
20.	Bread from heaven	1
21.	From slavery to Pharaoh in Egypt	1
22.	From slavery to sin	1
23.	They healed them	1
24.	No	1
25.	A covenant	1
26.	The blood of a sacrifice	1

Consult Bible for written Memory Work

If word perfect, 4 marks ... 4
(1 mark off for each mistake. If more
than 3 mistakes, no marks) TOTAL 33

60% – 20   75% – 25   90% – 30

STUDY NO. 5: A PROPHET LIKE MOSES

NOTES ON CORRECT ANSWERS

(The numbers in the lefthand margin correspond to the
numbers of the correct answers on the previous page.)

1-4. In each case, Satan, the great enemy of Israel, sought to destroy God's appointed deliverer before he could fulfill his task. Each was preserved through the faith and courage of his parents.

5. Both Moses and Jesus were equipped by God with special intellectual gifts.

6. Both relied on God's supernatural power, not on their own natural strength.

7-8. Wrong attitudes can keep God's people from recognizing or honoring the deliverer whom God has sent to them.

9-10. Both Moses and Jesus were willing to bear the punishment of God's people, but only Jesus could be accepted by God because He Himself was without sin (Heb. 7:26-27).

12-16. Both Moses and Jesus were dependent on personal communion with God. The results of this communion were manifested in various unique ways.

19. The name of God reveals the nature of God. Through Moses God revealed Himself as eternal and unchanging; through Jesus He revealed Himself as Father (see Matt. 11:27 Rom. 8:15).

20. The manna provided through Moses only sustained temporary, physical life. Some of those who ate it died later under God's judgment (Num. 14:22-23, 32; 26:63-65). But through Jesus, the believer receives eternal life (John 6:47-51).

21-22. The slavery from which Moses delivered Israel was physical; the slavery from which Jesus delivers the believer is spiritual.

25-26. Israel broke the first covenant which God made with them, but God promised to make a new covenant which would provide forgiveness of all their sins (Jer. 31:31-34). Jesus came to institute this new covenant.

CONCLUSION:

This study brings out 26 points of clear resemblance between Moses and Jesus. It would be impossible to find any other prophet who has arisen in Israel, except Jesus, who resembles Moses in even a small number of these points. Therefore, it is unreasonable to deny that Jesus is the prophet whom Moses foretold in Deut. 18:18-19.

However, if Jesus is the prophet whom Moses foretold, it is of the utmost importance for us to recognize this fact and act upon it. God said concerning this prophet: ". . . whoever will not hear My words, which He speaks in My name, I will require it of him."

The choice, then, is between the judgment of God or His blessing. Judgment if we reject Jesus, God's prophet; blessing if we acknowledge Him.

FIRST PROGRESS ASSESSMENT

CONGRATULATIONS!

You have now completed the FIRST FIVE STUDIES. Consider for a moment what this implies!

You have made a detailed analysis of some of the most profound and important themes ever unfolded in the world's literature. These include:

The history and destiny of Israel.

The lives and characters of three of the greatest men who have ever crossed the stage of human history: Abraham, Moses and Jesus.

The central theme of all biblical prophecy: the life and work of the Messiah-Redeemer.

In so doing, you have searched out for yourself in the Bible the answers to *more than 200 specific questions*.

You have also committed to memory *seven key verses of Scripture*.

Perhaps at times you may have found the going rough. You may have asked yourself: Is it really worth all the time and effort? But that only confirms what Solomon said about the search for wisdom: it is like digging for treasure buried in the earth.

Digging is hard, back-breaking work. It produces aching muscles and blistered hands. It is not strange, therefore, if you have experienced some mental "aches" and "blisters" as you have worked through these first five studies.

On the other hand, you are also developing mental and spiritual "muscles." You are building inner stamina and strength of character. The "aches" and the "blisters" are temporary – they will pass. But the character you are developing will be with you forever. It is an essential basis for future success, no matter what your walk in life.

So don't sacrifice the permanent for the sake of the temporary! Keep on digging! The treasure really is there. It will be yours when you have fulfilled the requirements.

FIRST REVIEW

Before you go on to the exciting new material that still lies before you, it will both encourage and strengthen you to take stock of all that you have discovered up to now. Here are some helpful ways to do this.

First, read carefully through all the questions of the preceding five studies together with the corresponding correct answers. Check that you now know and understand the correct answer to each question.

Second, review all the passages in these five studies which you have learned for Memory Work.

Third, read carefully through the following questions and consider how you would answer them. Each question is related in some way to the material you have been studying.

1. What lessons from the history of Israel would you say are still applicable to Israel and to other nations today?

2. What acts of mercy was Jesus empowered to do by the anointing of the Holy Spirit upon Him?

3. State ten incidents in the life of Jesus which fulfilled specific prophecies of the Old Testament.

4. State ten important points of resemblance between Moses and Jesus.

Finally, write out on a separate sheet of paper your own answer to any *one* of the above questions.

* * * * *

There are no marks allotted for this First Review. Its purpose is to help you *consolidate* all that you have been discovering. When you are satisfied that this has been achieved, turn the page to Study No. 6.

STUDY NO. 6

GOD'S REMEDY FOR SIN (Part 1)

Introduction:

The Bible diagnoses for us a disease of the human heart which is called sin. This consists of an inward spiritual attitude of rebellion toward God, which is expressed in outward acts of disobedience. All of us suffer from this disease, which is fatal if not dealt with. It produces three successive effects: first, inward spiritual death, or separation from God; second, the physical death of the body; third, eternal banishment from God's presence.

Messiah came to save us from our sins. Being without sin, He took our sins upon Himself, died in our place, and rose again from the dead, that we might be forgiven and receive eternal life.

Memory Work: Rom. 6:23   Please check when memory card prepared ☐

(Review daily Deut. 18:18)

A. SIN AND ITS CONSEQUENCES

1. What aspect of God's own character does He love in man? (Ps. 11:7)

2. What is the attitude of God toward wickedness? (Prov. 15:9)

3. What kind of person does God love? (Prov. 15:9)

4. Name seven things which God hates. (Prov. 6:16-19)

   (1).. (2)..

   (3)..

   (4)..

   (5)..

   (6).. (7)..

5. Name nine things which are an abomination to the Lord. (Deut. 18:10-12)

   (1)..

   (2).. (3)..

   (4).. (5)..

   (6).. (7)..

   (8).. (9)..

6. Are there any people who have not sinned? (Ps. 14:2-3)

7. Is there any man who never sins? (1 Kings 8:46)

8. Name two ways in which we have all committed iniquity. (Is. 53:6)

   (1)..

   (2)..

9. When men turned from God, what were the first two sins that they committed? (Rom. 1:21)

   (1).. (2)..

10. What were the results of this? (Rom. 1:21)

    (1) In their mind?..

    (2) In their heart?..

11. Write down two facts about the human heart. (Jer. 17:9)

    (1).. (2)..

12. Who alone knows the truth about the human heart? (Jer. 17:10)

13. Write down thirteen evil things which come out of the human heart. (Mark 7:21-22)

    (1).............................. (2).............................. (3)..............................

    (4).............................. (5).............................. (6)..............................

    (7).............................. (8).............................. (9)..............................

    (10)............................ (11)............................ (12)..............................

    (13)..............................

14. How do these things affect a man? (Mark 7:23)

15. If we are able to do something good and do not do it, what does God call that?
(1 Sam. 12:23   James 4:17)

16. If we say that we have no sin, what do we do to ourselves? (1 John 1:8)

17. If we say that we have not sinned, what do we do to God? (1 John 1:10)

18. How do even our best attempts at righteousness appear in God's sight? (Is. 64:6)

19. What are two things that separate us from God? (Is. 59:2)
(1)... (2)...

20. What consequence has sin brought upon all men? (Gen. 2:17   Ezek. 18:4, 20   Rom. 5:12; 6:23)

21. What is the present condition of those who are separated from God by their sins? (Eph. 2:1)

22. What is the end of those who are finally banished from God's presence? (Matt. 25:41   Jude 7)

23. What is the second death? (Rev. 20:14-15)

24. Write down eight kinds of people who will experience the second death. (Rev. 20:15; 21:8)
(1).. (2).. (3)..
(4).. (5).. (6)..
(7).. (8)..

B. THE PURPOSE OF MESSIAH'S DEATH AND RESURRECTION
25. For what purpose did Messiah come into the world? (1 Tim. 1:15)

26. Whom did Jesus call and whom did He receive? (Matt. 9:13   Luke 15:2)

27. Did Jesus Himself commit any sins? (Is. 53:9   Heb. 4:14-15   1 Pet. 2:22)

28. On account of what two things was Messiah wounded and bruised? (Is. 53:5)
(1)... (2)...

29. What did Messiah bear in His own body on the cross? (1 Pet. 2:24)

30. For what purpose did Messiah die? (1 Pet. 3:18)

31. What three facts about Jesus are the heart of the gospel? (1 Cor. 15:3-4)
(1)... (2)...
(3)...

32. Seeing that Messiah is now alive forevermore, what is He able to do for those who come to Him? (Heb. 7:25)

33. Write down three things now offered to all men in the name of Jesus. (Luke 24:47   Acts 4:12)
(1).. (2).. (3)..

Memory Work: Romans 6:23
Write out this verse from memory.

DO NOT TURN THIS PAGE UNTIL YOU HAVE COMPLETED ALL ANSWERS IN THIS STUDY

STUDY NO. 6: GOD'S REMEDY FOR SIN (Part 1)

CORRECT ANSWERS AND MARKS

Question No.	Answers	Marks
1.	Righteousness	1
2.	It is an abomination to God	1
3.	Him who follows righteousness	1
4.	(1) A proud look (2) A lying tongue (3) Hands that shed innocent blood	3
	(4) A heart that devises wicked plans (5) Feet that are swift in running to evil	2
	(6) A false witness (7) One who sows discord among brethren	2
5.	(1) One who makes son or daughter pass through the fire (demon worship)	1
	(2) One who practices witchcraft (3) A soothsayer (horoscopes)	2
	(4) One who interprets omens	1
	(5) A sorcerer (drugs, hypnosis)	1
	(6) One who conjures spells	1
	(7) A medium (consults familiar spirits)	1
	(8) A spiritist (9) One who calls up the dead (necromancer)	2
6.	None	1
7.	No	1
8.	(1) We have all gone astray (2) We have turned, every one, to his own way	2
9.	(1) They did not glorify God (2) They were not thankful	2
10.	(1) They became futile in their thoughts (2) Their foolish hearts were darkened	2
11.	(1) It is deceitful above all things (2) It is desperately wicked	2
12.	The Lord	1
13.	(1) Evil thoughts (2) Adulteries (3) Fornications (4) Murders (5) Thefts	5
	(6) Covetousness (7) Wickedness (8) Deceit (9) Licentiousness	4
	(10) An evil eye (11) Blasphemy (12) Pride (13) Foolishness	4
14.	They defile him	1
15.	Sin	1
16.	We deceive ourselves	1
17.	We make God a liar	1
18.	Like filthy rags	1
19.	(1) Our iniquities (2) Our sins	2
20.	Death	1
21.	Dead in trespasses and sins	1
22.	Eternal fire	1
23.	The lake of fire	1
24.	(1) The cowardly (2) The unbelieving (3) The abominable (4) Murderers	4
	(5) Sexually immoral (6) Sorcerers (7) Idolaters (8) All liars	4
25.	To save sinners	1
26.	Sinners	1
27.	No	1
28.	(1) Our transgressions (2) Our iniquities	2
29.	Our sins	1
30.	To bring us to God	1
31.	(1) He died for our sins (2) He was buried (3) He rose again the third day	3
32.	To save them to the uttermost	1
33.	(1) Repentance (2) Remission of sins (3) Salvation	3

Consult Bible for written Memory Work
If word perfect, 4 marks 4
(1 mark off for each mistake. If more
than 3 mistakes, no marks)   TOTAL $\overline{80}$

60% – 48   75% – 60   90% – 72

STUDY NO. 6: GOD'S REMEDY FOR SIN (Part 1)

NOTES ON CORRECT ANSWERS

(The numbers in the lefthand margin correspond to the
numbers of the correct answers on the previous page.)

1-3. Righteousness is primarily a right attitude of heart expressed by right actions. It is conformity to God's requirements and not to the standards of society, including religion. God loves true righteousness in man, but He is irrevocably opposed to wickedness.

4. Note that sowing discord is in the same category as shedding innocent blood.

5. All the practices here listed are in the realm of the "occult." Some contemporary examples are: Satan worship; Ouija board; fortune telling; drug abuse; mediums; clairvoyants; oriental cults (e.g. yoga); transcendental meditation; astrology; horoscopes; hypnosis; automatic writing; palmistry; grapho-analysis.

6-7. God's Word is absolutely clear: we have all sinned. There are no exceptions.

8. Turning to our own way is one sin of which we are all guilty. Our way is not God's way (see Is. 55:8-9).

9. All sin is first and foremost against God, although its consequences often affect other people also.

10. When men turn from God, they turn into darkness.

11-14. All these Scriptures speak about "the heart" generally. They describe the inward condition of all fallen humanity, without any exceptions.

15. Many people are guilty not so much for the evil that they do as for the good that they do not do.

16-17. God has already pronounced His verdict: "Guilty." It is futile to dispute it.

18. Our own efforts at righteousness cannot change the basic corruption of our hearts.

19-24. Separation from God brings immediate spiritual death, which leads eventually to the physical death of the body. God warned Adam that he would die the very day that he ate the forbidden fruit (Gen. 2:17). But Adam did not die physically for several hundred years (Gen. 5:5). Those who die in their sins will ultimately be confined to the lake of eternal fire, which is called "the second death."

25-26. God cannot condone sin, but He offers mercy to sinners.

27-30. By the Levitical sacrifices sin was temporarily "covered" from year to year (Lev. 16:29-30). But by the sacrifice of Jesus sin was finally "put away" (Heb. 9:26; 10:11-12). Thus the way is now open for man to turn back to God.

31. The gospel is not merely a theory or a philosophy. It is based on the facts of human history and verified in human experience.

32-33. The salvation which God offers us through Jesus is complete and eternal.

STUDY NO. 7

GOD'S REMEDY FOR SIN (Part 2)

Introduction:

God's offer of salvation under the New Covenant is to the individual. It is not based on ethnic background or inheritance, on religious practices or good works, but comes only through personal faith in Messiah's atoning death. To accept God's offer and receive salvation we must:

(1) acknowledge our sins and repent (turn from our sins),
(2) believe that Messiah died for us and rose again,
(3) receive the risen Messiah by faith as *personal* Savior,
(4) publicly confess Messiah as Lord.

When we have received Messiah as Savior and Lord, He comes to dwell continuously in our hearts and gives to us eternal life and the power to lead a life of righteousness and victory over sin.

Memory Work: John 1:12-13   Please check when memory card prepared ☐

(Review daily Rom. 6:23)

C. HOW WE MAY RECEIVE THE REMEDY

28. What is the condition of those who seek righteousness through the law but fail to keep it? (Deut. 27:26 Gal. 3:10)

29. Is it sufficient to keep all the law except for one commandment? (Deut. 4:2; 12:32 James 2:10-11)

30. Can we achieve righteousness with God by keeping the law? (Rom. 3:20)

31. Can we be saved by our own good works? (Eph. 2:8-9 Tit. 3:5)

32. If we trust in our own efforts to be righteous, what is our condition? (Jer. 17:5)

33. How did Abraham achieve righteousness with God? (Gen. 15:6 Rom. 4:20-22)

34. How may we achieve righteousness with God? (Rom. 4:23-24)

35. (a) Why was Jesus delivered to death? (Rom. 4:25)

(b) Why was Jesus raised from the dead? (Rom. 4:25)

36. What has God provided to atone for our sins? (Lev. 17:11)

37. What does the blood of Jesus do for us if we meet God's conditions? (1 John 1:7)

38. What must we do to find God? (Jer. 29:13)

39. If we desire mercy, what two things must we do? (Prov. 28:13)

(1).. (2)..

40. In order to receive salvation through faith in Jesus the Messiah, what two things must we do? (Rom. 10:9-10)

(1)..

(2)..

41. If we come to Messiah will He reject us? (John 6:37)

42. If we invite Messiah into our lives, what promise has He given us? (Rev. 3:20)

43. If we receive Messiah, what does He give us? (John 1:12)

44. What experience do we have as a result? (John 1:13; 3:3)

45. When we receive Messiah, what does God give us through Him? (Rom. 6:23)

46. Is it possible to know that we have eternal life? (1 John 5:13)

47. What record does God give us concerning the Messiah? (1 John 5:11)

48. If we have received Jesus the Messiah, the Son of God, what do we have? (1 John 5:12)

D. MESSIAH GIVES POWER TO OVERCOME THE WORLD AND SATAN

49. After we have received Jesus the Messiah, who lives in our hearts by faith? (Gal. 2:20 Eph. 3:17)

50. What can we do through the strength which Messiah gives us? (Phil. 4:13)

51. If we confess Jesus the Messiah before men, what will He do for us? (Matt. 10:32)

52. If we deny Jesus the Messiah before men, what will He do for us? (Matt. 10:33)

53. What kind of person is able to overcome the world and its temptations?
    (1) (1 John 5:4)
    (2) (1 John 5:5)
54. Why are God's children able to overcome the world? (1 John 4:4)

55. By what three things do the people of God overcome Satan? (Rev. 12:11)
    (1)
    (2)
    (3)
56. Whom has God promised to receive in heaven as His child? (Rev. 21:7)

Memory Work: John 1:12-13
Write out these verses from memory.

STUDY NO. 7: GOD'S REMEDY FOR SIN (PART 2)

CORRECT ANSWERS AND MARKS

Question No.	Answers	Marks
28.	They are under a curse	1
29.	No	1
30.	No	1
31.	No	1
32.	We are under a curse	1
33.	By believing in His promise	1
34.	By believing in Him who raised up Jesus our Lord	1
35.	(a) Because of our offenses (b) Because of our justification	2
36.	The blood on the altar	1
37.	It cleanses us from all sin	1
38.	Search for Him with all our hearts	1
39.	(1) Confess our sins (2) Forsake our sins	2
40.	(1) Confess with our mouth the Lord Jesus	1
	(2) Believe in our heart that God has raised Jesus from the dead	1
41.	No	1
42.	"I will come in"	1
43.	The right to become children of God	1
44.	We are born of God (born again)	1
45.	Eternal life	1
46.	Yes (John wrote for that purpose)	1
47.	God has given us eternal life in the Messiah	1
48.	Life (eternal)	1
49.	Messiah	1
50.	All things (that God wishes us to do)	1
51.	He will confess us before His heavenly Father	1
52.	He will deny us before His heavenly Father	1
53.	(1) The one who is born of God (through his faith)	1
	(2) The one who believes that Jesus is the Son of God	1
54.	Because the One in them (God) is greater than the one in the world (Satan)	1
55.	(1) By the blood of the Lamb (Jesus the Messiah)	1
	(2) By the word of their testimony	1
	(3) By not loving their lives to the death	1
56.	He who overcomes	1

Consult Bible for written Memory Work

If word perfect, 4 marks for each verse 8
(1 mark off for each mistake. If more than three mistakes
in either verse, no marks for that verse.)   TOTAL 43

60% – 26   75% – 32   90% – 39

STUDY NO. 7: GOD'S REMEDY FOR SIN (Part 2)

NOTES ON CORRECT ANSWERS

(The numbers in the lefthand margin correspond to the
numbers of the correct answers on the previous page.)

28-30. The purpose of the law was fourfold:

(1) To reveal God's standard of righteousness and man's sinful condition (Rom. 3:19-20).

(2) To prove the inability of men to make themselves righteous by their own efforts (Rom. 7:18-23).

(3) To foretell and foreshadow Messiah both through direct prophecy (Deut. 18:18-19) and through sacrifices and ordinances of the law (Ex. 12:3-7, 13).

(4) To keep Israel separate from the other nations, set apart to God's special purposes.

28,32. Deut. 28:15-68 gives a vivid picture of the results of being under a curse. God has provided only one way of freedom: through Jesus the Messiah (see Gal. 3:13-14).

28-32. The Bible rules out every attempt of man to save himself, or to make himself righteous, apart from the grace of God received through faith in the Messiah (see Hab. 2:4).

36-37. In both the Old and New Testaments, the shed blood of a sacrifice is the only basis for atonement of sins (Heb. 9:22).

39. Merely to "confess" sin without forsaking it does not procure for man the mercy of God. (Compare Is. 55:7.)

44. John 3:1-7 tells us that "we must be born again." John 1:12-13 tells us how we can be born of God. It is by receiving Jesus the Messiah as our personal Savior and Lord.

45. In Romans 6:23 notice the contrast: a) "wages" = the due reward for the sins we have committed; b) "gift" = the free, undeserved gift of God's grace.

49. The believer's life continues as it begins, "by faith." "As you have therefore received Messiah Jesus the Lord, so walk in Him . . ." (Col. 2:6). We received the Messiah by faith. We walk in the Messiah by faith (2 Cor. 5:7).

51-52. Jesus the Messiah is "the High Priest of our confession" (Heb. 3:1). His high-priestly ministry on our behalf is limited by the extent to which we "confess" Him. (Compare Heb. 4:14 and 10:21-23.) In the last resort, we have only two alternatives: to confess or to deny.

55. ". . . By the blood of the Lamb and by the word of their testimony" means that we testify personally to what the Word of God says that the blood of Messiah does for us. Here are some of the great benefits received through the blood of Christ:

1) redemption (Eph. 1:7)

2) cleansing (1 John 1:7)

3) justification (Rom. 5:9)

4) sanctification (Heb. 13:12)

56. Compare Romans 12:21. In the last resort, there are only two alternatives: either to overcome or to be overcome.

STUDY NO. 8

GOD'S PLAN FOR HEALING OUR BODIES (Part 1)

Introduction:

By turning away from God in disobedience, man lost the blessing and protection of God and came under a curse and the power of the devil. In this way, the devil was able to bring upon man's body many forms of pain and weakness and sickness. For this reason Messiah on the cross bore not only our sins but also our sicknesses. Therefore, by faith in Messiah we may now receive physical healing for our bodies, as well as forgiveness and peace for our souls.

Memory Work: Ps. 103:2-3   Please check when memory card prepared ☐
(Review daily John 1:12-13)

A. GENERAL: WHO BRINGS SICKNESS AND WHO BRINGS HEALTH?

1. Who first deceived man and tempted him to disobey God? (Gen. 3:1-13   1 John 3:8   Rev. 12:9)

2. Why did pain, sickness and death first come to man? (Gen. 3:16-19)

3. Who brought sickness upon Job? (Job 2:7)

4. Who brought sickness on the woman described in Luke 13:11-16? (v. 16)

5. With what did Satan bind her? (Luke 13:11)

6. What does God promise to do for His people who obey Him? (Ex. 15:26)

7. What two things does God promise to do for His people who serve Him? (Ex. 23:25)
   (1)
   (2)

8. Do sicknesses belong to God's people or to those who hate them? (Deut. 7:15)

9. What two things did David say the Lord did for him? (Ps. 103:3)
   (1)
   (2)

10. What three things did the apostle John wish for his friend who was a believer? (3 John 2)
    (1)   (2)
    (3)

11. How many of God's promises may we claim through faith in Messiah? (2 Cor. 1:19-20)

12. For what purpose was Messiah manifested to the world? (1 John 3:8)

13. For what purposes did God anoint Messiah with the Holy Spirit? (Acts 10:38)

14. Whose will did Jesus the Messiah come to do? (Ps. 40:7-8   John 5:30; 6:38)

....

15. Who worked Jesus' miracles in Him? (John 10:37-38; 14:10)

....

16. How many did Jesus heal of those who came to Him? (Matt. 8:16; 12:15; 14:35-36
    Luke 4:40; 6:19)

....

17. How many kinds of sickness did Jesus the Messiah heal? (Matt. 4:23-24; 9:35)

....

18. In the light of the answers to questions 14-17, is it God's will to heal His people?

....

19. When Jesus did not heal many people, what was the reason? (Matt. 13:58   Mark 6:5-6)

....

20. Does God ever change? (Mal. 3:6   James 1:17)

....

21. Does Messiah ever change? (Heb. 13:8)

....

B. THE PURPOSE OF MESSIAH'S DEATH ON THE CROSS

22. Mention three things which Messiah bore in our place. (Matt. 8:17   1 Pet. 2:24)
    (1).. (2)..
    (3)..

23. As a result, what three consequences can we have in our lives? (1 Pet. 2:24)
    (1).. (2)..
    (3)..

24. What was Messiah made for us? (Gal. 3:13)

....

25. From what has Messiah redeemed us? (Gal. 3:13)

....

26. How many kinds of sickness were included in the curse of the law?
    (Deut. 28:15, 21, 22, 27, 28, 35, 59-61)

....

27. Which should we choose? (Deut. 30:19)
    (1) Life or Death?..
    (2) Blessing or Curse? ....

Memory Work: Psalm 103:2-3
Write out these verses from memory.

....

....

....

....

....

DO NOT TURN THIS PAGE UNTIL YOU HAVE COMPLETED ALL ANSWERS IN THIS STUDY

STUDY NO. 8: GOD'S PLAN FOR HEALING OUR BODIES (Part 1)

CORRECT ANSWERS AND MARKS

Question No.	Answers	Marks
1.	The serpent, the Devil, Satan*	1
2.	Because man disobeyed God	1
3.	Satan	1
4.	Satan	1
5.	With a spirit of infirmity	1
6.	To put none of the diseases of Egypt upon them – to heal them	2
7.	(1) To bless their bread and water	1
	(2) To take sickness away from them	1
8.	To those who hate them	1
9.	(1) The Lord forgave all his iniquities	1
	(2) The Lord healed all his diseases	1
10.	(1) That he might prosper (2) That he might be in health	2
	(3) That his soul might prosper	1
11.	All God's promises	1
12.	To destroy the works of the devil	1
13.	To do good and heal all who were oppressed by the devil	2
14.	The will of God the Father	1
15.	God the Father	1
16.	All, every one	1
17.	All kinds of sickness and disease	1
18.	Yes	1
19.	The people's unbelief	1
20.	Never	1
21.	Never	1
22.	(1) Our infirmities (2) Our sicknesses (3) Our sins	3
23.	(1) We can be dead to sins	1
	(2) We can live for righteousness	1
	(3) By His (Messiah's) stripes we are healed	1
24.	A curse	1
25.	The curse of the law	1
26.	Every kind of sickness	1
27.	(1) Life (2) Blessing	2

Consult Bible for written Memory Work

If word perfect, 4 marks 8
(1 mark off for each mistake. If more than three mistakes
in either verse, no marks for that verse)   TOTAL $\overline{46}$

60% – 28   75% – 35   90% – 41

* "Serpent," "Devil," "Satan" are all different names for the same person. (See Rev. 12:9.)

STUDY NO. 8: GOD'S PLAN FOR HEALING OUR BODIES (Part 1)

NOTES ON CORRECT ANSWERS

(The numbers in the lefthand margin correspond to the
numbers of the correct answers on the previous page.)

1-2. Genesis chapter 3 reveals the root cause of all human sufferings and traces it back to the devil. Jesus Himself said of the devil: "He was a murderer from the beginning" (John 8:44).

3-5. If we trace all sickness back to its source, the devil is the sole author of it. It is part of "the works of the devil."

9. Note the repetition of "all" with both "iniquities" and "diseases."

10. Note that Gaius, to whom John wrote, was a model believer, "walking in the truth" and "doing faithfully" his duty as a believer (3 John 3-5).

11. Second Corinthians 1:20 rebuts dispensational theories which would rob believers of the benefits of physical healing in this present dispensation. "ALL" God's promises are (NOW) for "US" (= all believers). Applied personally: "Every promise that fits my situation and meets my need is for me now."

13. All three Persons of the Godhead are actively present in the ministry of healing. The FATHER anointed the SON with the SPIRIT. The result: healing for all. This was already foreshadowed in Isaiah 48:16.

13-15. The Messiah, Jesus, is the perfect manifestation of God the Father's will. This applies to healing as well as to all else that Jesus did.

16-17. There is no record in the Gospels of any person who came to Messiah for healing who was not healed.

20-21. The unchanging truth of the gospel is based on the unchanging nature of God Himself.

22. Both Matthew and Peter are here quoting Is. 53:4-5. The correct literal translation of Is. 53:4 is: "Surely He has borne our sicknesses and carried our pains." This refers to Messiah. In 1 Peter 2:24 the word translated "healed" is the basic Greek word for physical healing from which the Greek word for "doctor" is derived.

25. "The curse of the law" means the curse that results from the breaking of the law. This curse is fully described in Deut. 28:15-68. It includes every form of sickness.

27. God sets forth two opposite pairs: either (a) "life" and "blessing"; or (b) "death" and "cursing." It is left to man to choose.

STUDY NO. 9

GOD'S PLAN FOR HEALING OUR BODIES (Part 2)

Introduction:

Healing for our bodies comes to us from God through hearing and believing God's Word and through allowing God's Spirit to fill our bodies with the resurrection life of Messiah. Not only may we receive healing for our bodies in this way, but we may also offer healing and deliverance to others in the name of Jesus. Two main ways in which we may do this are by laying our hands on the sick and praying for them or by getting believing church elders to anoint them with oil in the name of the Lord. If we act in faith in this way, God will work with us and confirm the truth of His Word by miracles of healing and deliverance.

Memory Work: Mark 16:17-18   Please check when memory card prepared ☐
(Review daily Psalm 103:2-3)

C. THREE MEANS OF HEALING:

(1) God's Word   (2) God's Spirit   (3) Our Faith

28. What does God send to heal and deliver us? (Ps. 107:20)

....

29. Mention two things which God's words bring to His children. (Prov. 4:20-22)

(1).. (2)..

30. If God's Spirit dwells in us, what will it do for our mortal bodies? (Rom. 8:11)

....

31. What does God want to manifest in our mortal bodies? (2 Cor. 4:10-11)

....

32. What did Jesus look for in those who came to Him for healing? (Matt. 9:28-29   Mark 2:5; 9:23   Luke 8:50)

....

33. How did Peter explain the healing of a lame man? (Acts 3:16)

....

34. What did Paul perceive in the cripple at Lystra which enabled him to be healed? (Acts 14:8-10)

....

35. How does faith come to us? (Rom. 10:17)

....

D. THE AUTHORITY COMMITTED TO BELIEVERS

36. Mention two kinds of power which Jesus the Messiah gave to His disciples. (Matt. 10:1)

(1)..

(2)..

37. Mention four things which Jesus commanded His disciples to do. (Matt. 10:8)

(1).. (2)..

(3).. (4)..

38. When the disciples failed to heal an epileptic, what reason did Jesus give? (Matt. 17:20)

....

39. What two things did Jesus say that a person who believed in Him would be able to do? (John 14:12)

    (1).. (2)..

40. What may believers do for sick people in the name of Jesus? (Mark 16:17-18)

    ....

41. What will happen to such sick people? (Mark 16:18)

    ....

42. What should a sick believer do? (James 5:14)

    ....

43. What two things should church elders do for a sick believer? (James 5:14)

    (1)
    ....

    (2)..

44. What two things will the Lord do for such a believer? (James 5:15)

    (1).. (2)..

45. What kind of prayer will save the sick? (James 5:15)

    ....

46. What two things did the disciples pray that God would do in the name of Jesus? (Acts 4:30)

    (1)..

    (2)..

47. When the disciples went out and preached, what two things did the Lord do for them? (Mark 16:20)

    (1)..

    (2)..

Memory Work: Mark 16:17-18
Write out these verses from memory.

....

....

....

....

....

DO NOT TURN THIS PAGE UNTIL YOU HAVE COMPLETED ALL ANSWERS IN THIS STUDY

CORRECT ANSWERS AND MARKS

Question No.	Answers	Marks
28.	His (God's) Word	1
29.	(1) Life (2) Health to all their flesh	2
30.	It will give life to our mortal bodies	1
31.	The life of Jesus	1
32.	Faith	1
33.	Faith in the name of Jesus had healed him	1
34.	The cripple had faith to be healed	1
35.	By hearing the Word of God	1
36.	(1) Power over unclean spirits to cast them out	1
	(2) Power to heal all kinds of sickness and disease	1
37.	(1) To heal the sick (2) To cleanse the lepers	2
	(3) To raise the dead (4) To cast out demons	2
38.	Because of their unbelief	1
39.	(1) The works that He did (2) Greater works than these	2
40.	Believers may lay hands on the sick in the name of Jesus	1
41.	They will recover	1
42.	He should call for the elders of the church	1
43.	(1) Pray over him	1
	(2) Anoint him with oil in the name of the Lord	1
44.	(1) Raise him up (2) Forgive him if he has committed sins	2
45.	The prayer of faith	1
46.	(1) Stretch out His hand to heal	1
	(2) Grant signs and wonders to be done	1
47.	(1) The Lord worked with them	1
	(2) He confirmed the Word through the accompanying signs	1

Consult Bible for written Memory Work

If word perfect, 4 marks for each verse 8
(1 mark off for each mistake. If more than 3 mistakes
in either verse, no marks for that verse.)   TOTAL 38

60% – 23   75% – 29   90% – 34

STUDY NO. 9: GOD'S PLAN FOR HEALING OUR BODIES (Part 2)

NOTES ON CORRECT ANSWERS

(The numbers in the lefthand margin correspond to the
numbers of the correct answers on the previous page.)

28-34. Psalm 33:6 describes the means used by God in creation: "By the WORD of the Lord . . . and by the BREATH (= SPIRIT) of His mouth." All creation is by the WORD and the SPIRIT of God working together. The means by which we receive this work of healing is our FAITH.

29. Prov. 4:20-22. The alternative translation of "health" is "medicine." These verses are God's great "medicine bottle." However, this medicine must be taken according to the directions, which are fourfold: (1) "Give attention"; (2) "Incline your ear" (be humble and teachable); (3) "Do not let them depart from your eyes"; (4) "Keep them in the midst of your heart." The four channels to receive God's Word as medicine are the mind, the ear, the eye and the heart.

31. God's will is that the resurrection life of Messiah should be "manifested" (openly revealed) in our body. This is God's provision of healing, health and vitality for our bodies in this present life.

35. Rom. 10:17. First, God's Word produces "hearing." Then, out of "hearing" there develops "faith." The process of "hearing" is described in its four phases in Prov. 4:20-21.

36-37. In the New Testament no one is ever sent out to preach without also being commissioned to heal and to deliver from evil spirits. With Matt. 10:8 compare Matt. 28:20: "teaching them to observe all things that I have commanded you; and lo, I am with you always, even to the end of the age [this present age]." Messiah made provision that exactly the same ministry which He instituted with the first twelve disciples should be continued unchanged by each succeeding generation of disciples until the end of the present age.

39. The ministry of Jesus is the pattern for all His disciples. The Holy Spirit, sent by Jesus after He had returned to the Father, performs these works promised by Jesus through His believing disciples.

40. The promises of Mark 16:17-18 apply generally to "those who believe" – to all believers.

40-45. For further teaching on this subject, see Derek Prince's *Foundation Series*, Volume III, Book 5, *Laying On of Hands*.

42. A sick believer who does not call for the elders of the church is disobedient.

46. Acts 4:30 is still a pattern prayer for all believers.

STUDY NO. 10

THE BIBLE: THE WORD OF GOD

Introduction:

The Bible is God's own Word, His great gift to all men everywhere, to help them out of their sin and misery and darkness. The Bible is not an ordinary book, but the men who wrote it were inspired and moved by God's Holy Spirit to write exactly the truth as God gave it to them. Every word is true, filled with God's own power and authority. We should read our Bible as if it was God Himself speaking to us directly and personally. It will impart to us light, understanding, spiritual food and physical health. It will cleanse us, sanctify us, build us up, make us partakers of God's own nature. It will give us power and wisdom to overcome the devil.

Memory Work: 2 Tim. 3:16-17   Please check when memory card prepared ☐

(Review daily Mark 16:17-18)

1. What name did Jesus give to the Scripture? (John 10:35)

2. What did Jesus say about the Scripture which shows its authority? (John 10:35)

3. Write down two things which David tells us about God's Word.
   (1) (Ps. 119:89)
   (2) (Ps. 119:160)

4. How were the Scriptures originally given?
   (1) (2 Tim. 3:16)
   (2) (2 Pet. 1:20-21)

5. What kind of seed must a person receive into his heart in order to be born again and have eternal life? (1 Pet. 1:23)

6. Write down four things for which the Scriptures are profitable to a believer. (2 Tim. 3:16)
   (1)   (2)
   (3)   (4)

7. What is the final result in a believer who studies and obeys God's Word? (2 Tim. 3:17)

8. What is the spiritual food which God has provided for His people? (Deut. 8:3   Matt. 4:4   1 Pet. 2:2)

9. How much did Job esteem God's words? (Job 23:12)

10. When Jeremiah fed on God's Word, what did it become to him? (Jer. 15:16)

11. How can a young believer lead a clean life? (Ps. 119:9)

12. Why should a believer hide (store up) God's Word in his heart? (Ps. 119:11)

13. What two results does God's Word produce in young men when it abides in them? (1 John 2:14)

   (1)..

   (2)..

14. How did Jesus answer the devil each time He was tempted? (Matt. 4:4, 7, 10)

   ....

15. What is the sword which God has given to believers as part of their spiritual armor? (Eph. 6:17)

   ....

16. In what two ways does God's Word show believers how to walk in this world? (Ps. 119:105)

   (1)... (2)...

17. What two things does God's Word give to the mind of a believer? (Ps. 119:130)

   (1)... (2)...

18. What does God's Word provide for the body of a believer who studies it carefully? (Prov. 4:20-22)

   ....

19. When God's people were sick and in need, what did God send to heal and deliver them? (Ps. 107:20)

   ....

20. Write down four things, mentioned in the following verses, which God's Word does for His people.

   (1) (John 15:3   Eph. 5:26)...

   (2) (John 17:17)..

   (3) (Acts 20:32)..

   (4) (Acts 20:32)..

21. How does a believer prove his love for Messiah? (John 14:21)

   ....

22. Whom did Jesus call His mother and His brothers? (Luke 8:21)

   ....

23. How is God's love made perfect in a believer? (1 John 2:5)

   ....

24. Write down two results which follow in our lives when we claim the promises of God's Word. (2 Pet. 1:4)

   (1)..

   (2)..

Memory Work: 2 Timothy 3: 16-17

Write out these verses from memory.

....

....

....

....

....

STUDY NO. 10: THE BIBLE: THE WORD OF GOD

CORRECT ANSWERS AND MARKS

Question No.	Answers	Marks
1.	The Word of God	1
2.	It cannot be broken	1
3.	(1) It is settled forever in heaven	1
	(2) It is true in its entirety	1
4.	(1) By inspiration of God	1
	(2) Holy men of God spoke as they were moved by the Holy Spirit	2
5.	The incorruptible seed of God's Word	1
6.	(1) Doctrine (2) Reproof (3) Correction	3
	(4) Instruction in righteousness	1
7.	He is made complete, thoroughly equipped for every good work	2
8.	The Word of God	1
9.	More than his necessary food	1
10.	The joy and rejoicing of his heart	1
11.	By taking heed according to God's Word	1
12.	That he might not sin against God	1
13.	(1) It makes them strong	1
	(2) They overcome the wicked one (the devil)	1
14.	He answered from the written Word of God	1
15.	He answered from the written Word of God	1
16.	(1) It is a lamp to their feet (2) It is a light to their path	2
17.	(1) Light (2) Understanding	2
18.	Health to all his flesh	1
19.	His (God's) Word	1
20.	(1) It cleanses or washes like clean water	1
	(2) It sanctifies (3) It builds them up	2
	(4) It gives them their inheritance	1
21.	He has Messiah's commandments and keeps them	1
22.	Those who hear the Word of God and do it	1
23.	By keeping God's Word	1
24.	(1) We are made partakers of the divine nature	1
	(2) We escape the corruption of this world	1

Consult Bible for written Memory Work

If word perfect, 4 marks for each verse	8
(1 mark off for each mistake. If more than three mistakes in either verse, no marks for that verse.)	TOTAL 46

60% – 28   75% – 35   90% – 41

STUDY NO. 10: THE BIBLE: THE WORD OF GOD
NOTES ON CORRECT ANSWERS
(The numbers in the lefthand margin correspond to the
numbers of the correct answers on the previous page.)

1-2. The prophets of Israel, as well as the rabbis, have testified to the fact that the Old Testament is the Word of God. It is also clear that Jesus accepted the Old Testament Scriptures without question or reservation as the inspired, authoritative Word of God. He based all His teachings on these Scriptures and directed the whole course of His own life to obey and fulfill them.

    The New Testament is likewise revealed to be God's Word. In 2 Peter 3:15-16, Peter compares Paul's epistles to the Old Testament Scriptures. In 1 Tim. 5:18, Paul quotes from Luke 10:7 together with Deut. 25:4 indicating that Luke's writings are to be considered as authoritative as those of Moses. The book of Revelation ends with solemn warnings not to change any of the words therein, just as is recorded in Deut. 4:2. Moreover, Jesus promised that the Holy Spirit would both remind His disciples of what they had heard from Him and also lead them on into further truths that they would need. Therefore, the authority behind the New Testament, as behind the Old Testament, is that of the Holy Spirit (John 14:26; 16:13).

3. God's Word originates in heaven. Men were the channels through whom this Word was given, but God Himself is the source of it.

4. (1) "By inspiration of God" means literally "God inbreathed." The words "breath" and "spirit" are the same, both in Hebrew and Greek. (For a full study of the inspiration and authority of the Bible see Derek Prince's *Foundation Series*, Volume II, Book 1, *Foundation for Faith*.)

5. The "incorruptible seed" of God's Word, received by faith in the heart and caused to germinate there by the Holy Spirit, brings forth divine, eternal, incorruptible life.

6-8. Note: "ALL Scripture" (2 Tim. 3:16), "EVERY word" (Matt. 4:4). For full spiritual development, a believer must study and apply the teachings of the whole Bible.

8-10. God's Word provides food suited to every stage of spiritual development: (1) "milk" for newborn babes (1 Pet. 2:2); (2) "bread" for those growing up (Matt. 4:4); (3) "solid food" (full diet) for those who are "of full age" (spiritually mature) (Heb. 5:12-14).

11. "By taking heed according to Your word": i.e., by carefully applying the teaching of God's Word to every phase of his life.

12. Someone has said: "Either God's Word will keep you from sin, or sin will keep you from God's Word."

13-15. In Eph. 6:13-17, Paul lists six items of spiritual armor which provide the believer with complete protection, but of them all there is only one weapon of attack, "the sword of the Spirit." It is the responsibility of each believer to "take" this sword.

16. Compare 1 John 1:7: "If we walk in the light. . . ." "The light" by which we must walk is God's Word.

17-19. God's Word provides for the spirit, the mind and the body of the believer.

20. (4) Only through God's Word do we come to know what is our rightful inheritance in Messiah and how to obtain that inheritance.

21-23. ". . . The keeping of God's Word is the supreme distinguishing feature which should mark you out from the world as a disciple of Messiah."

    "Your attitude toward God's Word is your attitude toward God Himself. You do not love God more than you love His Word. You do not obey God more than you obey His Word. You do not honor God more than you honor His Word. You do not have more room in your heart and life for God than you have for His Word." (*Foundation Series*, Volume I, Book 1, *Foundation for Faith*, page 27.)

24. Through God's Word, believed and obeyed, God's own nature permeates the heart and life of the believer, replacing the old, corrupt, Adamic nature.

STUDY NO. 11

THE HOLY SPIRIT

Introduction:

The Holy Spirit was God's agent in creation and was the means by which He inspired and empowered men of God in the Old Testament period. Jesus, too, was anointed by God's Spirit and was completely dependent upon the Holy Spirit in all His earthly ministry.

Before the Holy Spirit descended upon Him at the river Jordan, He never preached a sermon or performed a miracle. After that, everything He did was by the power of the Holy Spirit. When He was about to leave His disciples, He promised that from heaven He would send the Holy Spirit to them (in their turn), to be their Helper and to supply all their spiritual needs. This promise was fulfilled at the feast of Pentecost (Hebrew: *Shavuot*) when they were all baptized in the Holy Spirit.

Memory Work: Acts 2:38-39   Please check when memory card prepared ☐

(Review daily 2 Tim. 3:16-17)

1. Who was hovering over the waters before God called light into being? (Gen. 1:2)

2. What worked together with God's Word to create the heavens and the earth? (Ps. 33:6)

3. What divine power made Elihu and gave him life? (Job 33:4)

4. How does God create and renew the face of the earth? (Ps. 104:30)

5. Who enabled the judges of Israel to deliver God's people? (Jud. 3:10; 6:34; 11:29; 14:6; 15:14-15)

6. How were the prophets empowered to proclaim the Word of the Lord? (Neh. 9:30 Micah 3:8   2 Pet. 1:21)

7. Who is joined with the Lord God in sending Messiah? (Is. 48:16)

8. What power enabled Messiah to fulfill His work of mercy? (Is. 61:1)

9. With what did God the Father anoint Jesus for His earthly ministry? (Acts 10:38)

10. What did John the Baptist see descend and abide upon Jesus? (John 1:32-33)

11. What did Jesus say was upon Him, enabling Him to preach and to minister to those in need? (Luke 4:18)

12. By what power did Jesus say He cast out demons? (Matt. 12:28)

13. Whom did Jesus say He would send to His disciples from the Father after He Himself returned to heaven? (John 14:16, 26; 15:26)

14. What two expressions does Jesus use to describe the Holy Spirit?
    (1) (John 14:17)
    (2) (John 14:26)

15. Write down two things which Jesus says the Holy Spirit will do for the disciples. (John 14:26)
    (1)
    (2)

16. Write down two other ways in which Jesus says the Holy Spirit will help the disciples. (John 16:13)
    (1)
    (2)

17. Write down two ways in which the Holy Spirit will reveal Jesus to His disciples.
    (1) (John 15:26)...
    (2) (John 16:14)...

18. After what did Jesus say that the disciples would receive power to become effective witnesses for Him? (Acts 1:8)
....

19. What did John the Baptist tell the people that Jesus would do for them? (Mark 1:8)
....

20. What promise did Jesus give to His disciples just before He ascended into heaven? (Acts 1:5)
....

21. What did Jesus tell His disciples to do until this promise should be fulfilled? (Luke 24:49)
....

22. Upon what day was this promise to these disciples fulfilled? (Acts 2:1-4)
....

23. Why could the Holy Spirit not be given to the disciples during the earthly ministry of Jesus? (John 7:39)
....

24. After Jesus had returned to His position of glory at the right hand of God, what did He receive from the Father? (Acts 2:33)
....

25. How could the unbelievers present know that Jesus had poured out the Holy Spirit upon His disciples? (Acts 2:33)
....

26. What could these unbelievers hear the disciples doing through the power of the Holy Spirit? (Acts 2:7-8)
....

27. Upon whom does God promise to pour out His Spirit at the close of this age?
    (Joel 2:28 [Joel 3:1 in the Hebrew Bible]   Acts 2:17)
....

28. To whom does Peter say that the promised gift of the Holy Spirit is made available? (Acts 2:39)
....

29. What good gift will God the Father give to all His children who ask Him for it? (Luke 11:13)
....

Memory Work: Acts 2:38-39

Write out these verses from memory.

....
....
....
....
....

DO NOT TURN THIS PAGE UNTIL YOU HAVE COMPLETED ALL ANSWERS IN THIS STUDY

STUDY NO. 11: THE HOLY SPIRIT

CORRECT ANSWERS AND MARKS

Question No.	Answers	Marks
1.	The Spirit of God	1
2.	The breath of God's mouth	1
3.	The Spirit of God	1
4.	He sends forth His Spirit	1
5.	The Spirit of the Lord	1
6.	They were empowered by the Spirit of the Lord	1
7.	The Spirit of the Lord God	1
8.	The Spirit of the Lord God	1
9.	With the Holy Spirit and with power	1
10.	The (Holy) Spirit	1
11.	The Spirit of the Lord	1
12.	By the Spirit of God	1
13.	Another Helper, the Holy Spirit	2
14.	(1) The Spirit of truth (2) The Helper	2
15.	(1) He will teach you all things	1
	(2) He will bring to your remembrance all things that I said to you	1
16.	(1) He will guide you into all truth	1
	(2) He will tell you things to come	1
17.	(1) He will testify of Me (Jesus) (2) He will glorify Me (Jesus)	2
18.	After the Holy Spirit has come upon you	1
19.	He will baptize you with the Holy Spirit	1
20.	You shall be baptized with the Holy Spirit not many days from now	1
21.	Tarry in the city of Jerusalem until you are endued with power from on high	2
22.	The Day of Pentecost (*Shavuot*)	1
23.	Because Jesus was not yet glorified	1
24.	The promise of the Holy Spirit	1
25.	They could see and hear it	1
26.	Speaking in the tongues (languages) of the countries in which the unbelievers had been born	2
27.	On all flesh	1
28.	To you and to your children, and to all who are afar off, as many as the Lord our God will call	2
29.	The Holy Spirit	1

Consult Bible for written Memory Work

If word perfect, 4 marks for each verse 8
(1 mark off for each mistake. If more than three mistakes
in either verse, no marks for that verse.)

TOTAL 45

60% – 27   75% – 34   90% – 41

STUDY NO. 11: THE HOLY SPIRIT

NOTES ON CORRECT ANSWERS

(The numbers in the lefthand margin correspond to the
numbers of the correct answers on the previous page.)

1-4. All three Persons of the Godhead were active in creation.

5-6. The Spirit of the Lord came upon men of God in the Old Testament period to give supernatural strength, wisdom, and authority to perform specific tasks. In the New Testament, however, the Holy Spirit comes to dwell permanently in the one who believes in Jesus (John 14:16-17).

7-13. The Old Testament prophets spoke many times of a coming Messiah, or one anointed by the Spirit of the Lord, who would save God's people. In historical perspective, Jesus became the "Messiah," the "anointed One," when the Holy Spirit descended and abode upon Him after His baptism by John the Baptist. The title "Messiah" indicates that the whole earthly ministry of Jesus was made possible by the "anointing" of the Holy Spirit. It is God's purpose that the same "anointing" of the Holy Spirit should be the abiding portion of all believers. "Now He who establishes us with you in Messiah and has anointed us is God" (2 Cor. 1:21). "But the anointing which you have received from Him abides in you . . ." (1 John 2:27). The Hebrew word translated "Messianic" and the Greek word translated "Christian" both mean literally "anointed one." To serve God effectively, the disciple is as much dependent upon the Holy Spirit as Jesus was.

13-14. "Helper" = "Advocate" – "One called in alongside." The same word is used of Jesus in 1 John 2:1. Messiah pleads the cause of the believer in heaven. The Holy Spirit, through the believer, pleads the cause of the Messiah on earth (see Matt. 10:19-20).

14-17. In John 16:7 Jesus said, "It is to your advantage that I go away; for if I do not go away, the Helper will not come to you; but if I depart, I will send Him to you." When Jesus returned to heaven and sent the Holy Spirit upon the disciples, they immediately received a better knowledge and understanding of Jesus Himself than they had had all the time that He was actually present with them on earth. Thus the Holy Spirit fulfilled His ministry to reveal, interpret and glorify the person, the work and message of Messiah.

19. John the Baptist's introduction of Jesus as "the baptizer in the Holy Spirit" is placed at the forefront of all four Gospels. The New Testament places the greatest possible emphasis upon this aspect of Messiah's ministry. All believers should do the same.

20-21. The Gospels close, as they open, with the promise of the baptism in the Holy Spirit.

23-24. By His death on the cross, Jesus purchased for every believer the gift of the Holy Spirit (see Gal. 3:13–14). After His resurrection and ascension, it was His unique privilege to receive this gift from the Father and to bestow it upon His disciples.

25-26. All through the New Testament the baptism in the Holy Spirit is attested by the supernatural evidence of speaking with other tongues.

26-29. At the close of this age God has promised a final, worldwide outpouring of the Holy Spirit. Every believer has the scriptural right to ask for this gift.

STUDY NO. 12

SUPERNATURAL POWER FOR GOD'S SERVICE

Introduction:

The baptism in the Holy Spirit is a supernatural enduement with power from heaven to equip the believer for effective witness and service. It is attested by speaking in a language given by the Holy Spirit but unknown to the one speaking. It enables the believer to build up his own spiritual life by direct and continual communion with God and is the gateway into a life in which both the gifts and the fruits of the Holy Spirit should be manifested. In the New Testament church, this experience was considered normal for all believers.

Memory Work: Joel 2:28-29   Please check when memory card prepared ☐
        Joel 3; 1-2 in Hebrew Bible
                (Review daily Acts 2:38-39)

1. According to Isaiah 28:9-11, how will the Lord speak to His people?

   ....

2. What supernatural endowment of speech did Jesus promise to those who believe in Him? (Mark 16:17)

   ....

3. What happened to the disciples on the Day of Pentecost (*Shavuot*) when they were all filled with the Holy Spirit? (Acts 2:4)

   ....

   ....

4. Through whose preaching did the people of Samaria come to believe in Jesus as Messiah? (Acts 8:12)

   ....

5. When Peter and John came down to Samaria, how did they pray for the believers there? (Acts 8:15)

   ....

6. How did the believers at Samaria receive the Holy Spirit? (Acts 8:17)

   ....

7. How did Saul of Tarsus (Paul) receive the Holy Spirit? (Acts 9:17)

   ....

8. As Peter was preaching to the people in the house of Cornelius, what happened to all who heard him? (Acts 10:44)

   ....

9. How did Peter and his companions know that all these people in the house of Cornelius had received the Holy Spirit? (Acts 10:45-46)

   ....

10. What question did Paul ask the disciples at Ephesus? (Acts 19:2)

   ....

11. How did these disciples at Ephesus receive the Holy Spirit? (Acts 19:6)

   ....

12. What happened after the Holy Spirit came on these disciples? (Acts 19:6)

   ....

13. How much did Paul say that he himself spoke in tongues? (1 Cor. 14:18)

   ....

14. Write down three things that a believer does when he speaks in an unknown tongue. (1 Cor. 14:2, 4)

(1).. (2)..

(3)..

15. If a believer prays in an unknown tongue, what part of him is then praying? (1 Cor. 14:14)

....

16. How did Jesus say that true worshipers should worship God? (John 4:23-24)

....

17. How does Jude exhort believers to build themselves up in their faith? (Jude 20)

....

18. When a believer speaks in an unknown tongue, what may he pray for next? (1 Cor. 14:13)

....

19. In a public meeting where there is no interpreter, how may a believer speak in an unknown tongue? (1 Cor. 14:28)

....

20. Did Paul say that he wished that all believers spoke in tongues? (1 Cor. 14:5)

....

21. How many believers did Paul say may prophesy? (1 Cor. 14:31)

....

22. Should believers be ignorant about spiritual gifts? (1 Cor. 12:1)

....

23. Make a list of the nine gifts of the Spirit. (1 Cor. 12:8-10)

(1).. (2)..

(3).. (4)..

(5).. (6)..

(7).. (8)..

(9)..

24. Make a list of the ninefold fruit of the Spirit. (Gal. 5:22-23)

(1)........................ (2)........................ (3)........................

(4)........................ (5)........................ (6)........................

(7)........................ (8)........................ (9)........................

25. Is it possible for a believer to have spiritual gifts without spiritual fruit? (1 Cor. 13:1-2)

....

26. Is it possible for a believer to have spiritual fruit without spiritual gifts? (1 Cor 12:31; 14:1)

....

27. Write down three supernatural occurrences that will result from the outpouring of the Holy Spirit at the end of this age. (Joel 2:28 [Joel 3:1 in the Hebrew Bible] Acts 2:17)

(1).. (2)..

(3)..

28. Write down five different spiritual contributions that a believer may make at a meeting with fellow believers. (1 Cor. 14:26)

(1)........................ (2)........................ (3)........................

(4)........................ (5)........................

Memory Work: Joel 2:28-29 (Joel 3:1-2 in the Hebrew Bible)
Write out these verses from memory.

....

....

....

....

....

DO NOT TURN THIS PAGE UNTIL YOU HAVE COMPLETED ALL ANSWERS IN THIS STUDY

STUDY NO. 12: SUPERNATURAL POWER FOR GOD'S SERVICE

CORRECT ANSWERS AND MARKS

Question No.	Answers	Marks
1.	With stammering lips and another tongue	1
2.	They will speak with new tongues	1
3.	They began to speak with other tongues as the Spirit gave them utterance	2
4.	The preaching of Philip	1
5.	That they might receive the Holy Spirit	1
6.	They (i.e. Peter and John) laid their hands on them	1
7.	Ananias laid his hands on him	1
8.	The Holy Spirit fell upon all of them	1
9.	They heard them speak with tongues and magnify God	1
10.	"Did you receive the Holy Spirit when you believed?"	1
11.	Paul laid hands on them	1
12.	They spoke with tongues and prophesied	1
13.	More than you all (i.e. more than all the believers at Corinth)	1
14.	(1) He speaks to God (not to men) (2) He speaks mysteries	2
	(3) He edifies himself	1
15.	His spirit	1
16.	In spirit and truth	1
17.	By praying in the Holy Spirit	1
18.	That he may interpret	1
19.	He may speak to himself and to God	1
20.	Yes	1
21.	All	1
22.	No	1
23.	(1) The word of wisdom (2) The word of knowledge	2
	(3) Faith (4) Gifts of healings (5) Working of miracles	3
	(6) Prophecy (7) Discerning of spirits	2
	(8) Different kinds of tongues (9) Interpretation of tongues	2
24.	(1) Love (2) Joy (3) Peace	3
	(4) Longsuffering (5) Kindness (6) Goodness	3
	(7) Faithfulness (8) Gentleness (9) Self-Control	3
25.	Yes	1
26.	Yes	1
27.	(1) Your sons and your daughters shall prophesy	1
	(2) Your old men shall dream dreams	1
	(3) Your young men shall see visions	1
28.	(1) A psalm (2) A teaching (3) A tongue	3
	(4) A revelation (5) An interpretation	2

Consult Bible for written Memory Work

If word perfect, 4 marks for each verse 8
(1 mark off for each mistake. If more than three mistakes
in either verse, no marks for that verse.)

TOTAL 61

60% – 37   75% – 46   90% – 55

STUDY NO. 12: SUPERNATURAL POWER FOR GOD'S SERVICE

NOTES ON CORRECT ANSWERS

(The numbers in the lefthand margin correspond to the
numbers of the correct answers on the previous page.)

1-2. The supernatural ability to speak in unknown tongues and to interpret them are the only manifestations of the Holy Spirit not found in the Old Testament. The remaining seven gifts of the Holy Spirit (1 Cor. 12:8-10) all appear in the Old Testament, as well as in Jesus' ministry.

3. "Out of the abundance of the heart the mouth speaks" (Matt. 12:34). The first outflow of the Holy Spirit is from the believer's mouth.

4-6. Through the ministry of Philip, multitudes in Samaria had been wonderfully saved and healed. But this was not sufficient for the apostles. They expected all new converts to receive the baptism in the Holy Spirit. This came to these converts in Samaria through the ministry of Peter and John, as a separate experience, subsequent to salvation.

7. Laying on of hands to impart the Holy Spirit was not confined to the apostles. Ananias is merely called a "disciple" (Acts 9:10). Nor is laying on of hands always needed to impart the Holy Spirit. In Acts 2:2-4 and 10:44-46 the believers received without any laying on of hands.

10-12. At Ephesus, as at Samaria, these disciples received the baptism in the Holy Spirit as a separate experience, subsequent to salvation. As in Acts 2:4 and 10:46, their experience culminated in speaking with other tongues (and also, in this case, prophesying).

13-17. After receiving the baptism in the Holy Spirit, the primary use of speaking in another tongue is for personal worship and prayer. The believer does not understand with his mind what he is saying, but his spirit holds direct communion with God, and in this way he is able to edify (build up) himself.

18-19. Through the gift of interpretation, believers may come to know the meaning of an utterance previously given in an unknown tongue. In public meetings an utterance given out loud in an unknown tongue should normally be followed by the interpretation. If there is no one to interpret, the believer may speak in an unknown tongue "to himself and to God."

21. To "prophesy" is to speak by the supernatural inspiration of the Holy Spirit in a language understood by the speaker and by those spoken to.

23-26. There is an important logical distinction between "gifts" and "fruit." A gift is imparted and received by a momentary act. Fruit is cultivated by time and labor (see 2 Tim. 2:6). In the life of the believer, the gifts of the Spirit are not a substitute for the fruit of the Holy Spirit, and the fruit is not a substitute for the spiritual gifts.

27-28. The full outpouring of the Holy Spirit always produces a variety of supernatural manifestations. Through these, believers are able to minister to one another on a level higher than that of natural ability or education.

SECOND PROGRESS ASSESSMENT

Once again, CONGRATULATIONS!

You have completed the FIRST TWELVE STUDIES – two-thirds, that is, of the total course.

The first five studies centered around the most important event in human history up to this time: *the atonement of Jesus*. Its outlines were foreshadowed by the prophets of the Old Testament. Then all the vivid details were filled in by the writers of the New Testament.

Now, in the seven studies which you have just completed, you have focused on the *marvelous benefits* which the atonement of Jesus obtained for the whole human race. You have studied in detail God's remedy for the two basic problems of humanity: sin and sickness. You have seen how wonderful and how complete the remedy is.

Think of it! You now have the answer, not merely for your own deepest needs, but for countless others who are struggling and suffering just as you were. You are no longer part of the problem, you are part of the solution! You can be a light to those around you in darkness.

What a tremendous responsibility! Left to yourself, you could never meet such a challenge. But God has not left you to yourself. He has made full provision for you to lead a life that reflects His grace and glory in every circumstance.

In studies 10, 11, and 12, you have been shown the double provision which God offers you: *His Word and His Spirit*. You have discovered how the Word and the Spirit, working together, can equip you for the new life which has opened up to you in the Messiah. Ask God to show you how to avail yourself of this provision in every area of your life.

Now just a word about what lies ahead. Studies 13, 14 and 15 deal with three important practical aspects of the new life. Then studies 16, 17 and 18 lead you on to the great climax of all history: *the personal return of the Messiah*.

Finally, study 19 brings all the strands together in a Personal Application.

SECOND REVIEW

Before you go on to these new studies, however, you need to check that you have fully mastered all the rich material contained in studies 6 through 12. The better you understand these, the better you will be able to grasp the exciting new material that lies ahead.

The method followed in this Second Review is similar to that of the first.

First, read carefully through all the questions of the preceding seven studies, together with the corresponding correct answers. Check that you now know and understand the correct answer to each question.

Second, review all the passages in these seven studies which you have learned for Memory Work.

Third, read carefully through the following questions and consider how you would answer them. Each question is related in some way to the material you have been studying.

> 1. How have you applied God's remedy for sin in your own life?

> 2. What scriptural reasons can you give to believe that God still heals those who trust Him today?

> 3. What benefits can you expect in your own life as you study and obey God's Word?

> 4. Describe different ways in which the Holy Spirit can help you in your spiritual life.

Finally, write out on a separate sheet of paper your own answer to any *one* of the above questions.

* * * * *

There are no marks allotted for this Second Review. Its purpose is to help you *consolidate* all that you have been discovering. When you are satisfied that this has been achieved, turn the page to Study No. 13.

STUDY NO. 13

WATER BAPTISM: HOW? WHEN? WHY?

Introduction:

Baptism has always played an important part in Judaism. The temple priests were required to purify themselves with water before performing their duties. Naaman, the Syrian, was cleansed from leprosy by immersing himself seven times in the Jordan. The Essenes, a Jewish sect, practiced ritual immersion for cleansing, and Judaism today still enjoins ritual immersion in water (the *Mikvah*). John the Baptist immersed those who returned to God in repentance, and even Jesus Himself was baptized as an act of obedience to the Father. In the New Testament, baptism is an essential step and was usually carried out immediately after one believed in Jesus. Jesus said, "He that believes and is baptized shall be saved" (Mark 16:16). God's way of salvation is still the same: first, believe; then be baptized. Believing in Christ produces an inward change in our hearts; being baptized in water is an outward act of obedience by which we testify of the change that has taken place in our hearts. By this act, we make ourselves one with Messiah in His burial and in His resurrection; we are separated from the old life of sin and defeat; and come out of the water to lead a new life of righteousness and victory, made possible by God's power in us. The Scriptures in this study explain very carefully how, when and why we must be baptized.

Memory Work: Rom. 6:4   Please check when memory card prepared ☐

(Review daily Joel 2:28-29 [Joel 3:1-2 in the Hebrew Bible])

1. What reason did Jesus Himself give for being baptized? (Matt. 3:15)

   ....

2. How did the Holy Spirit show that He was pleased with the baptism of Jesus? (Matt. 3:16)

   ....

3. What did God the Father say about Jesus when He was baptized? (Matt. 3:17)

   ....

4. Did Jesus go down into the water to be baptized? (Matt. 3:16)

   ....

5. If a person wishes to be saved, what did Jesus say he should do after believing the gospel? (Mark 16:16)

   ....

6. What did Jesus tell His disciples to do to people before baptizing them? (Matt. 28:19)

   ....

7. To whom did Jesus send His disciples with this message? (Matt. 28:19)

   ....

8. What does Jesus expect people to do after being baptized? (Matt. 28:20)

   ....

9. What did Peter tell people to do before being baptized? (Acts 2:38)

   ....

10. How many people did Peter say should be baptized? (Acts 2:38)

    ....

11. How did the people act who gladly received God's Word? (Acts 2:41)

    ....

12. What did the people of Samaria do after they believed Philip's preaching? (Acts 8:12)

    ....

13. After Cornelius and his friends had been saved and had received the Holy Spirit, what did Peter command them to do next? (Acts 10:44-48)

....

14. What did the Philippian jailer and his family do after believing Paul's message? (Acts 16:29-33)

....

15. What did the disciples at Ephesus do after believing Paul's message? (Acts 19:4-5)

....

16. (a) Write down three conditions a person must fulfill in order to be baptized.

    (1) (Acts 2:38)..

    (2) (Mark 16:16   Acts 8:12)..

    (3) (Matt. 28:19)..

  (b) Is an infant capable of fulfilling these three conditions?

....

17. Through what two experiences do believers follow Messiah Jesus when they are baptized? (Rom. 6:4   Col. 2:12)

  (1)...   (2)..

18. After being baptized, how can a believer answer God's requirements for righteousness? (1 Pet. 3:21)

....

19. How does Paul say believers should live after being baptized? (Rom. 6:4)

....

20. Is there any difference between believers of different races being baptized? (Gal. 3:26-28)

....

21. Mention two pictures of water baptism found in the Old Testament and referred to in the New Testament.

  (1) (1 Cor. 10:1-2   Ex. 14:21-22)

....

  (2) (1 Pet. 3:20-21   Gen. ch. 6 & 7)

....

Memory Work: Romans 6:4

Write out this verse from memory

....

....

....

DO NOT TURN THIS PAGE UNTIL YOU HAVE COMPLETED ALL ANSWERS IN THIS STUDY

STUDY NO. 13: WATER BAPTISM: HOW? WHEN? WHY?

CORRECT ANSWERS AND MARKS

Question No.	Answers	Marks
1.	". . . Thus it is fitting for us to fulfill all righteousness."	1
2.	He descended like a dove and alighted upon Him	1
3.	"This is My beloved Son, in whom I am well pleased."	1
4.	Yes	1
5.	He should be baptized	1
6.	To make disciples of them	1
7.	To all the nations	1
8.	To observe all things which He has commanded	1
9.	To repent	1
10.	Every one	1
11.	They were baptized	1
12.	They were baptized	1
13.	To be baptized	1
14.	They were baptized	1
15.	They were baptized	1
16.	(a) (1) He must repent	1
	(2) He must believe	1
	(3) He must become a disciple	1
	(b) No	1
17.	(1) His burial (2) His resurrection	2
18.	With a good conscience toward God	1
19.	They should walk in newness of life	1
20.	None	1
21.	(1) The Israelites passing through the Red Sea	1
	(2) Noah and his family passing through the flood in the Ark	1

Consult Bible for written Memory Work

If word perfect, 4 marks 4
(1 mark off for each mistake. If more than
three mistakes, no marks.)   TOTAL 30

60% – 18   75% – 23   90% – 27

STUDY NO. 13: WATER BAPTISM: HOW? WHEN? WHY?

NOTES ON CORRECT ANSWERS

(The numbers in the lefthand margin correspond to the
numbers of the correct answers on the previous page.)

1-4. Although Jesus was baptized by John the Baptist, He was not in the same class as all the others whom John baptized. John's baptism was a "baptism of repentance" accompanied by confession of sin (Mark 1:4-5). But Jesus had no sins to confess or repent of. Rather, by being baptized in this way, Jesus set a pattern for all who would afterward follow Him in obedience to the will of God. This is indicated by the reason which Jesus gave: ". . . thus it is fitting for us to fulfill all righteousness."

"Thus" establishes the manner of baptism: going down into, and coming up out of, the water. "It is fitting for us" establishes a precedent, which it becomes all sincere believers to follow. "To fulfill all righteousness" establishes the reason: to complete all righteousness. First, the believer is made righteous through his faith in Messiah. Then, in being baptized, he completes this inward righteousness of faith by the outward act of obedience. Thus understood, this ordinance of baptism has the openly expressed approval of all three Persons of the Godhead: Father, Son and Spirit. (For a full study of this subject, see chapter 2 of Derek Prince's *Foundation Series*, Volume I, Book 3, *From Jordan to Pentecost*.)

5, 6, 9, 16. Before being baptized, a person should fulfill the following three conditions: (1) be taught the nature of and the reason for the act; (2) repent of his sins; (3) believe in Jesus the Messiah as the Son of God.

7, 10-15. Jesus told His disciples that this ordinance of baptism was to be for "all nations." There were to be no exceptions. In fulfillment of this, the New Testament record shows that all new converts were always baptized without delay. In most cases this took place on the actual day of conversion. Never was there any lengthy delay between conversion and baptism. There is no reason that this pattern should not be followed now, just as in the early church.

8, 17, 19. By baptism, believers publicly identify themselves with Messiah in His burial and resurrection. After baptism, they are required to lead a new life of righteousness, made possible by the grace and power of the Holy Spirit.

18. He may have a good conscience towards God because he has done all that God requires of him.

21. (a) A double baptism for God's people is presented in 1 Cor. 10:1-2: "in the cloud and in the sea." Baptism "in the cloud" typifies baptism in the Holy Spirit. Baptism "in the sea" typifies water baptism. The children of Israel were saved from the death angel by the blood of the Passover lamb. Afterwards, passing through the Red Sea, they were separated from their past of bondage and became God's redeemed people.

(b) By faith Noah and his family entered into the Ark (= Messiah). Then, in the Ark, they passed through the water of the flood (= baptism). They were thus saved from God's judgment; separated from the old, ungodly world; and ushered into a completely new life.

STUDY NO. 14

GOD'S WITNESSES

Introduction:

God chose Israel to be a light to the nations. He also commanded His people to be witnesses of His salvation to the ends of the earth. By His atoning death on the cross, Jesus has made salvation possible for all men everywhere. But in order to receive salvation, each person must first hear the Word of God and the testimony of Jesus. God's plan is that every person who comes to know Messiah should be filled with the Holy Spirit and should then use this power to witness to others. In this way the testimony of Messiah should be continually extended until it has reached the uttermost part of the earth and until all nations have heard. This is the great way in which all believers can work together to prepare the way for the return of Messiah. Believers who are faithful in witnessing will receive a reward from Messiah Jesus Himself and will have the joy of seeing, in heaven, those who repented and received salvation through their testimony. Believers who are unfaithful will have to answer to God for the fate of the people to whom they failed to witness.

Memory Work: Acts 1:8   Please check when memory card prepared ☐
                              (Review daily Rom. 6:4)

1. What did the Lord say His people were to be for Him? (Is. 43:12)

2. To what extent does God want His salvation to reach? (Is. 49:6)

3. Name three Israelites from the Old Testament whom God chose to be His witnesses. (Is. 6:8-10 Jer. 1:4-7 Jonah 1:1-3; 3:1-3)
   (1)................................ (2) .... (3)................................

4. What did Jesus tell His disciples that they were to be for Him? (Acts 1:8)

5. How far did Jesus say that the witness of His disciples was to extend? (Acts 1:8)

6. To whom must the witness be extended before the end of this age? (Matt. 24:14)

7. Of what three things concerning Jesus did Peter say that he and the other disciples were witnesses? (Acts 10:39-41)
   (1)................................ (2) ....
   (3)................................

8. What did God tell Paul that he was to do for Messiah? (Acts 22:15)

9. What did Paul continue to do from the day that he came to know Jesus? (Acts 26:22)

10. What does a true witness do by his testimony? (Prov. 14:25)

11. What should a wise believer seek to do? (Prov. 11:30)

12. After Andrew found Jesus, whom did he in turn bring to Jesus? (John 1:35-42)

13. After Jesus found Philip, whom did Philip in turn bring to Jesus? (John 1:43-47)

14. When the Pharisees questioned the man born blind, what did he answer from his own experience? (John 9:25)

....

15. What two things should we talk about and make known to other people? (1 Chron. 16:8-9)

(1).. (2)..

16. When people opposed Paul's testimony in Corinth, what did God tell Paul? (Acts 18:9)

....

17. What spirit did Paul tell Timothy was not from God? (2 Tim. 1:7)

....

18. What does the fear of man bring? (Prov. 29:25)

....

19. What instruction did Paul give Timothy concerning the testimony of Messiah? (2 Tim. 1:8)

....

20. When Peter and John were commanded not to speak about Jesus, what two answers did they give?

(1) (Acts 4:20)...

(2) (Acts 5:29)...

21. When the other disciples heard that Peter and John had been forbidden to speak about Jesus, what did they all do? (Acts 4:24)

....

22. After the disciples had prayed and been filled with the Holy Spirit, what did they all do? (Acts 4:31)

....

23. What special position did God give Ezekiel among his people? (Ezek. 3:17)

....

24. What did God tell Ezekiel would happen to him if he failed to warn the sinners? (Ezek. 3:18)

....

25. What two things did Paul testify to all men at Ephesus? (Acts 20:21)

(1)..

(2)..

26. Why could Paul say he was pure from the blood of all men at Ephesus? (Acts 20:26-27)

....

....

27. What is the final reward laid up for all faithful witnesses of Messiah? (2 Tim. 4:8)

....

Memory Work: Acts 1:8
Write out this verse from memory.

....
....
....

DO NOT TURN THIS PAGE UNTIL YOU HAVE COMPLETED ALL ANSWERS IN THIS STUDY

– 65 –

STUDY NO. 14: GOD'S WITNESSES

CORRECT ANSWERS AND MARKS

Question No.	Answers	Marks
1.	Witnesses	1
2.	To the ends of the earth	1
3.	(1) Isaiah (2) Jeremiah (3) Jonah	3
4.	Witnesses	1
5.	To the end of the earth	1
6.	To all the nations	1
7.	(1) All that He did (2) His death (3) His resurrection	3
8.	To be His witness to all men of what he had seen and heard	1
9.	Witnessing both to small and great that the words of the prophets and Moses had been fulfilled	2
10.	He delivers souls	1
11.	To win souls	1
12.	Andrew found his brother, Simon Peter	1
13.	Philip found Nathanael	1
14.	"One thing I know: that though I was blind, now I see."	2
15.	(1) God's deeds (2) His wondrous works	2
16.	"Do not be afraid, but speak. . . ."	1
17.	A spirit of fear	1
18.	A snare	1
19.	Do not be ashamed of the testimony of our Lord	1
20.	(1) "We cannot but speak the things which we have seen and heard."	1
	(2) "We ought to obey God rather than men."	1
21.	They all prayed to God with one accord	1
22.	They spoke the word of God with boldness	1
23.	A watchman	1
24.	God would require their blood at his hand	1
25.	(1) Repentance toward God	1
	(2) Faith toward our Lord Jesus the Messiah	1
26.	Because he had not shunned to declare to them the whole counsel of God	1
27.	A crown of righteousness	1

Consult Bible for written Memory Work

If word perfect, 4 marks	4
(1 mark off for each mistake. If more than three mistakes, no marks.)	TOTAL 40

60% – 24   75% – 30   90% – 36

STUDY NO. 14: GOD'S WITNESSES

NOTES ON CORRECT ANSWERS

(The numbers in the lefthand margin correspond to the
numbers of the correct answers on the previous page.)

1. The present trend in Judaism against spreading the message of the God of Israel is relatively new. At the time of Jesus, the Pharisees were extremely zealous in their efforts to convert Gentiles to Judaism (see Matt. 23:15). God had always called Israel to be a "light to the Gentiles" and a witness to Himself in the midst of a pagan world.

2. Believers are not intended to be witnesses primarily to a doctrine, an experience, or a denomination, but to MESSIAH HIMSELF. Jesus said, "And I, if I am lifted up from the earth, will draw all peoples to Myself" (John 12:32). The believer's testimony should uplift Jesus. To do this effectively, it must be directed and empowered by the Holy Spirit.

7. Compare Acts 1:21-22 and 4:33. The central fact of all testimony concerning Messiah is His RESURRECTION from the dead.

8-9. Paul's testimony is a pattern for all believers. It was based on personal experience; it pointed to Messiah; it confirmed the record of the Scriptures.

10-11. Faithful personal testimony is the most effective way to bring other people to a personal knowledge of the Messiah.

12-13. Although Peter later became the acknowledged leader among the apostles and the chief preacher, it was his brother Andrew who first came to Messiah and then brought Peter in turn. Later, Philip in the same way brought Nathanael. Thus the pattern of individual soul-winning is set by the apostles themselves.

14. Someone has said: "The man with an experience is not at the mercy of the man with an argument."

15. A believer's conversation should be positive, glorifying God, and building his own faith and that of others.

16-19, 22. The greatest hindrance to effective testimony is "the spirit of fear" (timidity). The Bible teaches clearly that this spirit does not come from God and that a believer should not allow himself to be ensnared or bound by it. The remedy is to be filled with the Holy Spirit.

20. (2) Where there is a clear-cut choice between obedience to God and obedience to man, this answer of Peter and John is just as valid today.

21. Prayer is the great weapon given to believers to break down the barriers to their testimony.

23-26. Like Ezekiel in the Old Testament, Paul in the New Testament understood that he would be held accountable by God for those to whom he had been given opportunity to testify. He understood also that he was required by God to "keep back nothing," but to declare "all the counsel of God." God still requires the same of believers today.

STUDY NO. 15

GOD'S PLAN FOR PROSPERITY

Introduction:

All through the Bible God promises to bless and prosper those who trust and serve Him. In order to receive God's financial and material blessings, we must learn to follow God's rule of faith, which says, "Give, and it will be given to you . . ." (Luke 6:38). We begin by giving back to God the first tenth of all that we receive, in money or in produce. Over and above this "tithe," we bring our "offerings" to God, as the Holy Spirit directs us. As we do this in faith, God abundantly blesses us and supplies all our needs.

Memory Work: Matt. 6:33 Please check when memory card prepared ☐

(Review daily Acts 1:8)

A. EXAMPLES OF GOD'S SERVANTS WHO HAVE PROSPERED

1. When God gave Abraham victory in battle, what did Abraham give back to God's priest, Melchizedek? (Gen. 14:19-20)

....

2. How did God in turn deal with Abraham? (Gen. 24:1)

....

3. What three things did Jacob want God to do for him? (Gen. 28:20)

   (1).. (2)..

   (3)..

4. What did Jacob promise to give God in return? (Gen. 28:22)

....

5. How did God in turn deal with Jacob? (Gen. 33:11)

....

6. What kind of man was Joseph? (Gen. 39:2)

....

7. What was the reason for Joseph's prosperity? (Gen. 39:2, 23)

....

8. What three things did God command Joshua concerning His law? (Josh. 1:8)

   (1)..

   (2)..

   (3)..

9. What did God promise Joshua if he would do these three things? (Josh. 1:8)

....

....

10. What did David promise Solomon if he would obey all the statutes and judgments of God's law? (1 Chron. 22:13)

....

11. As long as Uzziah sought the Lord, what did God do for him? (2 Chron. 26:5)

....

12. When Hezekiah sought and served God with all his heart, what happened to him? (2 Chron. 31:21; 32:30)

....

B. CONDITIONS AND PROMISES OF PROSPERITY

13. Concerning a certain kind of person, God says that "whatever he does shall prosper" (Ps. 1:3).
    (a) Write down three things that such a person MUST NOT do. (Ps. 1:1)
        (1)...
        (2)...
        (3)...
    (b) Write down two things that such a person MUST do. (Ps. 1:2)
        (1)...
        (2)...

14. In what two ways did God say that Israel had been robbing Him? (Mal. 3:8)
    (1).. (2)..

15. What happened to Israel as a result of robbing God? (Mal. 3:9)
    ....

16. How did God tell Israel to "prove" Him (i.e., put Him to the test)? (Mal. 3:10)
    ....

17. What did God promise Israel that He would then do for them? (Mal. 3:10)
    ....

18. What two things does Messiah tell His disciples to seek before all others? (Matt. 6:33)
    (1).. (2)..

19. What result does Messiah promise will then follow? (Matt. 6:33)
    ....

20. When we give, with what measure will it be given back to us? (Luke 6:38)
    ....

21. By what standard did Paul tell each believer to measure how much he should set aside for God? (1 Cor. 16:2)
    ....

22. For what purpose did Messiah become poor? (2 Cor. 8:9)
    ....

23. What kind of person does God love? (2 Cor. 9:7)
    ....

24. If we wish to reap bountifully, what must we do first? (2 Cor. 9:6)
    ....

25. If God's grace abounds towards us, what two results will follow? (2 Cor. 9:8)
    (1)...
    (2)...

26. From what kind of people will God withhold no good thing? (Ps. 84:11)
    ....

27. What kind of people will not want (lack) any good thing? (Ps. 34:10)
    ....

28. What will God supply to those who give liberally like the Philippian saints? (Phil. 4:19)
    ....

Memory Work: Matthew 6:33
Write out this verse from memory

....

....

....

STUDY NO. 15: GOD'S PLAN FOR PROSPERITY
CORRECT ANSWERS AND MARKS

Question No.	Answers	Marks
1.	A tithe of all	1
2.	God blessed Abraham in all things	1
3.	(1) Be with him (2) Keep him in the way that he went	2
	(3) Give him bread to eat and clothing to put on	1
4.	A tenth of all that God would give him	1
5.	God dealt graciously with Jacob	1
6.	Joseph was a successful man	1
7.	The Lord was with him and made what he did to prosper	1
8.	(1) It should not depart from his mouth	1
	(2) He should meditate in it day and night	1
	(3) He should observe to do according to all that is written in it	1
9.	God would make his way prosperous and he would have good success	1
10.	Then you will prosper	1
11.	God made him prosper	1
12.	He prospered in all his works	1
13.	(a) (1) NOT walk in the counsel of the ungodly	1
	(2) NOT stand in the path of sinners	1
	(3) NOT sit in the seat of the scornful	1
	(b) (1) He MUST delight in the law of the Lord	1
	(2) He MUST meditate in it day and night	1
14.	(1) In tithes (2) In offerings	2
15.	The whole nation was cursed with a curse	1
16.	By bringing all the tithes into the storehouse	1
17.	Open the windows of heaven and pour out such blessing that there would not be room enough to receive it.	2
18.	(1) The kingdom of God (2) The righteousness of God	2
19.	All the material things that they need will be added to them	1
20.	With the same measure that we measure with	1
21.	By how much he himself had prospered	1
22.	That we through His poverty might become rich	2
23.	A cheerful giver	1
24.	We must sow bountifully	1
25.	(1) We shall always have all sufficiency in all things	1
	(2) We shall have an abundance for every good work	1
26.	Those who walk uprightly	1
27.	Those who seek the Lord	1
28.	He will supply all our need according to His riches in glory by Messiah Jesus	2

Consult Bible for written Memory Work

If word perfect, 4 marks   4
(1 mark off for each mistake. If more
than three mistakes, no marks.)   TOTAL 46

60% – 28   75% – 35   90% – 41

STUDY NO. 15: GOD'S PLAN FOR PROSPERITY

NOTES ON CORRECT ANSWERS

(The numbers in the lefthand margin correspond to the
numbers of the correct answers on the previous page.)

1-5. Note that the practice of "tithing" did not begin with the law of Moses. The first person recorded in the Bible as giving tithes is Abraham. In Rom. 4:11-12 Abraham is called "the father of all those who believe . . . who also walk in the steps of the faith which our father Abraham had . . ." Believers who give their tithes to God today are certainly "walking in the steps of the faith of Abraham." Note also that the priest to whom Abraham gave tithes was Melchizedek. In Hebrews ch. 5, 6 and 7, it is shown that Messiah is our great "High Priest after the order of Melchizedek." In this capacity, He still receives the tithes of His believing people. Both Abraham and Jacob experienced God's material blessings as a result of their tithing. In Gen. 32:10 Jacob says, "I crossed over this Jordan with my staff, and now I have become two companies." When Jacob started to give tithes to God, he owned nothing but the staff in his hand. Twenty years later he was the prosperous head of a large and flourishing household.

6-7. Outward circumstances cannot prevent God from keeping His promises. Even in the prison Joseph prospered. Much more so, when he became prime minister of Egypt. Joseph's prosperity was the outworking of his character and his relationship to God.

8-9. Joshua was called to lead God's people into "the promised land." Today believers are called to enter "a land of promises." Then or now, the conditions for success are the same. Note especially the importance of right meditation. Compare the answer to question 13(b) (2).

10-12. From David to the Babylonian captivity, God prospered every king of Judah who was obedient to the law and faithful in the service of the temple.

13. Note that Ps. 1:1-3 does not describe one particular historical character but applies generally to every believer who fulfills the conditions stated.

14-15. Unfaithfulness by God's people in giving to God can bring a national curse. The principle still applies today.

16-21. The only basis of righteousness acceptable to God is FAITH. "Whatever is not from faith is sin" (Rom. 14:23). (Compare Heb. 11:6.) This principle applies in our financial dealings as much as in every other part of our life.

22. According to the Bible, poverty is a curse. Deut. 28:15-68 lists all the curses that result from breaking God's law. In verse 48 the following are included: "Therefore you shall serve your enemies . . . in hunger, in thirst, in nakedness, and in need of all things." This is absolute poverty. On the cross Messiah took upon Himself every one of these curses (see Gal. 3:13-14). He was hungry, thirsty, naked, in need of all things. He did this that believers might in return receive God's abundant provision for every need (see Phil. 4:19).

23. "Cheerful"; literally, "hilarious."

24. Believers should give in the same way that a farmer sows seed – carefully, intelligently, in the area calculated to yield the best returns for God's kingdom.

26-28. Prosperity is God's will for His believing, obedient people.

STUDY NO. 16

THE SECOND COMING OF MESSIAH

Introduction:

   When Messiah Jesus first came to earth nearly 2000 years ago, His coming exactly fulfilled in every detail all the prophecies of the Bible relating to that event. When He left this earth to return to heaven, He promised His disciples very definitely that He would come back to the earth again. Apart from these promises which Jesus Himself gave, there are many prophecies throughout the whole Bible concerning the second coming of Messiah, an event which will mark the establishment of God's kingdom over all the earth. In fact, there are even more prophecies of Jesus' second coming than there are about His first coming. Since the prophecies of His first coming were exactly and literally fulfilled, it is reasonable to believe that the prophecies of His second coming will be fulfilled in the same way. The Scriptures in this study contain the clear promises of Messiah's return. They also tell us what will happen to believers at that time, and how believers must in the meanwhile prepare themselves.

Memory Work: Luke 21:36   Please check when memory card prepared ☐
(Review daily Matt. 6:33)

A. PROPHECIES OF MESSIAH'S COMING TO RULE

1. Of what shall the earth one day be full? (Is. 11:9)

2. According to Daniel's vision, who was to come with the clouds of heaven and receive an everlasting kingdom? (Dan. 7:13-14)

3. (1) What did Jesus call Himself? (Matt. 24:27)

   (2) In what way did He say He would return? (Matt. 24:30)

4. For what purpose did Jesus say He was leaving His disciples? (John 14:2)

5. What promise did Jesus give His disciples when He left them? (John 14:3)

6. When Jesus was taken up into heaven, what promise did the angels give? (Acts 1:11)

7. When Messiah comes to rule, on what will He stand? (Zech. 14:4)

8. What is the "blessed hope" to which all true believers look forward? (Tit. 2:13)

9. What three sounds will be heard when Messiah descends from heaven? (1 Thess. 4:16)
   (1)_____   (2)_____
   (3)_____

B. WHAT WILL HAPPEN TO BELIEVERS

10. Will all believers have died when Messiah comes? (1 Cor. 15:51)

11. At this time what will happen to believers who have died? (1 Thess. 4:16)

12. Write down two things that will then happen to all believers, whether they have died or not.
   (1) (1 Cor. 15:51)_____
   (2) (1 Thess. 4:17)_____

13. Will these believers ever again be separated from the Lord? (1 Thess. 4:17)

....

14. When we actually see the Lord, what change will take place in us? (1 John 3:2)

....

15. As a result of this change, what will the body of the believer then be like? (Phil. 3:21)

....

16. What two words does Paul use to describe the body of the believer after resurrection? (1 Cor. 15:53)

(1).. (2)..

17. What name does the Bible give to the feast which believers will then enjoy? (Rev. 19:9)

....

C. HOW BELIEVERS MUST PREPARE

18. What did the Lamb's wife do before the marriage supper? (Rev. 19:7)

....

19. What kind of clothing did she wear? (Rev. 19:8)

....

20. What does the fine linen represent? (Rev. 19:8)

....

21. Of the ten virgins, which ones went in to the marriage? (Matt. 25:10)

....

22. If a man has the hope of seeing the Lord when He comes, how does he prepare himself for this? (1 John 3:3)

....

23. To whom will Messiah appear the second time for salvation? (Heb. 9:28)

....

24. What two things must we follow after, if we desire to see the Lord? (Heb. 12:14)

(1).. (2)..

25. Write down three conditions which should mark out all believers at Messiah's coming. (2 Pet. 3:14)

(1).. (2).. (3)..

26. What expression does Messiah use to show how sudden His coming will be? (Rev. 3:3; 16:15)

....

27. Who knows the day and hour of Messiah's coming? (Mark 13:32)

....

28. What did Jesus warn all believers to do in view of His coming? (Mark 13:35-37)

....

29. What did Jesus warn believers to do in addition to watching? (Luke 21:36)

....

30. What three things did Jesus warn could keep believers from being ready? (Luke 21:34)

(1).. (2).. (3)..

Memory Work: Luke 21:36
Write out this verse from memory.

....

....

....

DO NOT TURN THIS PAGE UNTIL YOU HAVE COMPLETED ALL ANSWERS IN THIS STUDY

STUDY NO. 16: THE SECOND COMING OF MESSIAH

CORRECT ANSWERS AND MARKS

Question No.	Answers	Marks
1.	The earth shall be full of the knowledge of the Lord as the waters cover the sea	2
2.	One like the Son of Man	1
3.	(1) The Son of Man	1
	(2) On the clouds of heaven with power and great glory	2
4.	To prepare a place for them	1
5.	"I will come again and receive you to Myself"	1
6.	This same Jesus will so come in like manner as you saw Him go into heaven	2
7.	The Mount of Olives	1
8.	The Glorious appearing of our great God and Savior Jesus the Messiah	2
9.	(1) A shout (2) The voice of an archangel	2
	(3) The trumpet of God	1
10.	No	1
11.	They will rise first (from the dead)	1
12.	(1) They will all be changed	1
	(2) They will all be caught up in the clouds to meet the Lord in the air	1
13.	Never	1
14.	We shall be like Him	1
15.	Like the glorious (glorified) body of Messiah	1
16.	(1) Incorruption (2) Immortality	2
17.	The marriage supper of the Lamb (Messiah)	1
18.	She made herself ready	1
19.	Fine linen, clean and bright	1
20.	The righteous acts of the saints	1
21.	Those who were ready	1
22.	He purifies himself even as He (Messiah) is pure	2
23.	To those who eagerly wait for Him	1
24.	(1) Peace with all men (2) Holiness	2
25.	(1) In peace (2) Without spot (3) Blameless	3
26.	"As a thief"	1
27.	Only God the Father	1
28.	To watch	1
29.	To pray always	1
30.	(1) Carousing (gluttony) (2) Drunkenness	2
	(3) Cares of this life	1

Consult Bible for written Memory Work

If word perfect, 4 marks   4
(1 mark off for each mistake. If more
than 3 mistakes, no marks)   TOTAL 49

60% – 29   75% – 37   90% – 44

STUDY NO. 16: THE SECOND COMING OF MESSIAH

NOTES ON CORRECT ANSWERS

(The numbers in the lefthand margin correspond to the
numbers of the correct answers on the previous page.)

1-4. The Bible clearly indicates that there will come an age where God's kingdom will be established on earth. This time period will be characterized by righteousness, peace and justice among all nations. The Messiah Jesus, the seed of David, will usher in that glorious age when He returns to judge the nations and save His people. His kingdom is described in Psalm 72.

3-8. ". . . That 'by the mouth of two or three witnesses every word may be established'" (Matt. 18:16, etc.). Concerning the return of Messiah we have the three witnesses: (1) Messiah Himself (John 14:3); (2) the angels (Acts 1:11); (3) the apostle Paul (1 Thess. 4:16). Note the emphasis on the return of Messiah IN PERSON: "THIS SAME Jesus . . ." "the Lord HIMSELF . . ." This "blessed hope" is the supreme goal of every believer's life.

9. (1) The shout will come from the Lord Himself, for His voice alone has power to call forth the dead (see John 5:28-29). (2) The archangel will presumably be Gabriel, whose special duty is to announce impending interventions of God in the affairs of men (see Dan. 9:21-22 Luke 1:19, 26). (3) The trumpet is used to call God's people together (Num. 10:2-3).

10. To "sleep" means to die (compare Acts 7:60 1 Cor. 11:30). This word is particularly used of the death of believers because they look forward to "waking" again on the resurrection morning.

11-12. The following order of events is indicated: (1) Dead believers will be resurrected with new, glorified bodies. (2) Living believers will have their bodies instantaneously changed to similar, glorified bodies. (3) All believers will be caught up together in clouds to meet the Lord as He descends from heaven.

17. Compare Matt. 8:11; 26:29.

18-25, The Bible very clearly teaches that, in order to be ready for the return of Messiah,
28,29. believers will have to prepare themselves diligently. According to Rev. 19:8, they will be clothed with "the righteous acts of the saints." This is the practical outworking in the believer's life of the righteousness of Messiah received by faith. (Compare Phil. 2:12-13: "work out . . . for it is God who works in you.") The main requirements of God's Word in this respect may be summarized as follows: (1) Purity (without spot) (1 John 3:3 2 Pet. 3:14); (2) Holiness (Heb. 12:14); (3) Peace (= right relations with all men) (Heb. 12:14 2 Pet. 3:14); (4) Blamelessness (= faithfulness in every duty of the believer) (2 Pet. 3:14); (5) Expectancy (Heb. 9:28); (6) Watchfulness (Mark 13:37); (7) Prayerfulness (Luke 21:36).

26. The Messiah will be "like a thief" in the manner of His coming, but He will take only that which is His own. It is "those who are Messiah's at His coming" (1 Cor. 15:23).

27. When the moment comes, the Father will tell the Son. Then all heaven will be stirred to action.

30. (1) Messiah always warned against "gluttony" BEFORE "drunkenness." (3) Compare Luke 17:27–28. The things mentioned here are not sinful in themselves. The sin consists in becoming absorbed in them.

STUDY NO. 17

THE LAST DAYS AND MESSIAH'S RETURN

Introduction:

The Bible tells us of various things which will be happening in the world at the time just before Messiah's second coming. It also tells which signs indicate that He will be coming soon. This study is divided into two parts. In Section A, some of the scriptural signs of Messiah's return are stated. The Scripture references for these signs are given below. The student is required to do the following:

(1) Read through the signs in Section A.

(2) Read through the Scriptures of which the references are given below Section A.

(3) On the dotted line below each sign, write in the reference of the Scripture which mentions that sign. (Some Scriptures refer to more than one sign.)

(4) At the end of each sign, you will see a square box ☐ When you have finished the entire section, read through the signs once again, and check each box if you feel that that particular sign is being fulfilled in the world as you know it today.

Section B consists of questions regarding God's plan and purpose for Israel as revealed in the prophetic Scriptures. After reading the Scripture reference, the correct answer is to be written in the blank space, as in previous lessons.

Memory Work: Luke 21:28   Please check when memory card prepared ☐

(Review daily Luke 21:36)

A. SIGNS OF MESSIAH'S RETURN

1. Great international wars ☐

....

2. Increase of travel and knowledge ☐

....

3. Worldwide outpouring of the Holy Spirit ☐

....

4. Many scoffers, denying the Word of God and the promises of Messiah's return ☐

....

5. Abounding iniquity (lawlessness) ☐

....

6. Great decline in moral and ethical standards, combined with outward
   forms of religion ☐

....

7. People absorbed in material pleasure and pursuits and forgetting the impending
   judgments of God (as in the days before the Flood and before the destruction of Sodom
   and Gomorrah) ☐

....

8. Many false prophets ☐

....

9. A great falling away from biblical faith ☐

....

10. Famines and pestilences ☐

....

11. Increase in severity and frequency of earthquakes ☐

....

12. Worldwide proclamation of the Gospel of Jesus the Messiah ☐

....

Joel 2:28 (Joel 3:1 Hebrew Bible)   Matthew 24:11   Matthew 24:7
Acts 2:17   Matthew 24:14   Daniel 12:4
2 Peter 3:2-7   Luke 17:26-30   Matthew 24:12
2 Timothy 3:1-5   2 Thess. 2:3

B. ISRAEL IN PROPHECY

13. According to the prophetic Scriptures, what would happen to the people of Israel if they continued in disobedience to God? (Deut. 28:63-67 Ezek. 36:19 Luke 21:24)

....

14. Does this mean that God has irrevocably cast away the Jewish people? (Jer. 31:35-37 Rom. 11:1)

....

15. After scattering Israel among all nations, what does the Lord say He will do for His people? (Jer. 16:14-15 Ezek. 36:24)

....

....

16. After the return of the Jewish people to the land of Israel, what will happen (Ezek. 36:35) to the:

    (1) desolate land?...

    (2) waste cities?...

17. According to Jesus, what city will be liberated from Gentile dominion in the time period immediately preceding His return to earth? (Luke 21:24)

....

18. What period does the psalmist predict in God's timetable? (Ps. 102:13)

....

19. During this period, what will Jerusalem become to all peoples? (Zech. 12:3)

....

20. What will the Lord do when Israel's enemies gather against Jerusalem at the end of the age? (Zech. 14:3)

....

....

21. During the period of the restoration of the Jews to the land of Israel, what two things does God promise to give to His people? (Ezek. 36:26)

    (1)...   (2)...

22. What great event will happen at this time to the whole remnant of the Jewish people? (Rom. 9:27; 11:26)

....

23. Name three things that we can all do to take part in God's work of redemption of Israel? (Jer. 31:7, 10 Is. 40:1-2)

    (1)..

    (2)..

    (3)..

Memory Work: Luke 21:28

Write out this verse from memory

....

....

....

DO NOT TURN THIS PAGE UNTIL YOU HAVE COMPLETED ALL ANSWERS IN THIS STUDY

STUDY NO. 17: THE LAST DAYS AND MESSIAH'S RETURN

CORRECT ANSWERS AND MARKS

Question No.	Answers	Marks
1.	Matthew 24:7	1
2.	Daniel 12:4	1
3.	Joel 2:28 (Joel 3:1 in Hebrew Bible) Acts 2:17	1
4.	2 Peter 3:2-7	1
5.	Matthew 24:12	1
6.	2 Timothy 3:1-5	1
7.	Luke 17:26-30	1
8.	Matthew 24:11	1
9.	2 Thess. 2:3	1
10.	Matthew 24:7	1
11.	Matthew 24:7	1
12.	Matthew 24:14	1
13.	They would be scattered among all peoples	1
14.	No	1
15.	He will gather them out of all countries and will bring them into their own land	2
16.	(1) The desolate land will become like the Garden of Eden	1
	(2) The waste cities will be fortified and inhabited	1
17.	Jerusalem	1
18.	A time for God to have mercy and favor on Zion	1
19.	Jerusalem will become a very heavy stone	1
20.	The Lord will go forth and fight against them as He fights in the day of battle	2
21.	(1) A new heart (2) A new spirit	2
22.	The whole remnant will be saved	1
23.	(1) Pray for the salvation of Israel	1
	(2) Declare (proclaim) the regathering of Israel	1
	(3) Comfort the Jewish people	1

Consult Bible for written Memory Work

If word perfect, 4 marks (1 mark off for each mistake. If more than 3 mistakes, no marks)	4
	TOTAL 33

60% – 20   75% – 25   90% – 30

STUDY NO. 17: THE LAST DAYS AND MESSIAH'S RETURN

NOTES ON CORRECT ANSWERS

(The numbers in the lefthand margin correspond to the
numbers of the correct answers on the previous page.)

1. This century has seen wars greater and more numerous than any preceding century, especially the two World Wars.

2. Note how these two factors are logically connected. The increase in knowledge (science) has made possible the increase in travel. Likewise, the increase in travel contributes to the increase of knowledge.

3. The expression "all flesh" denotes the entire human race. It is often used with this meaning in the prophets. (See Is. 40:5 Jer. 25:31 Ezek. 21:4-5.) Every section of the human race will feel the impact of this last great outpouring of God's Spirit.

4. The past century has witnessed systematic attacks on the Bible such as no previous century can record. Paradoxically enough, these attacks on the Bible are actually confirmations of its accuracy since the Bible clearly predicts them.

5-7. These signs are attested daily by the newspapers of the modern world. (Compare Luke 17:26 with Gen. 6:5, 12-13.) The three main evil features of Noah's day were: (1) evil imaginations; (2) sexual corruption and perversion; (3) violence.

8-9. These two signs indicate a tremendous increase towards the close of this age in satanic deception. The enormous rise in cults as well as the rejection of biblical truth by religious leaders are signposts that the Messiah Jesus is returning soon.

10. Famines and pestilences naturally tend to accompany each other and both are often caused by war. With the world populations growing faster than the food supply, starvation and sickness are growing more and more common.

11. Records over the past century indicate a marked increase in the frequency of earthquakes.

12. Evangelistic outreach is the natural outcome of the outpouring of God's Spirit. Radio and other contemporary media have now made it possible to reach all peoples with the message of the Messiah. Note the special comment after this sign: ". . . And then the end will come."

13. One continuing purpose behind the Lord's judgments on Israel has been to cause His people to return to Himself (see also Amos 4:6–12).

14. A central character trait of God is His covenant faithfulness to Israel, despite her unfaithfulness to Him. God's commitment to His covenant with Israel should be an encouragement to all who follow the Messiah.

15. There are numerous Scriptures which declare that God has given the land of Israel to the Jewish people. Years of dispersion have not changed that fact. (See Amos 9:15 Gen. 17:7-8; 26:3-4; 35:11-12.)

16. The building up of an industrially and agriculturally self-sufficient democracy in what was once a desolate land is a modern day miracle.

17. Jerusalem was recaptured by Israel in the Six Day War of 1967, but the Temple area remained in Arab (Gentile) hands.

18. The rise of Zionism and the rebirth of Israel are signs that the time to favor Zion has come.

19. The central issue of contention in the Arab/Israeli conflict is the status of Jerusalem.

20. At the return of the Messiah, God Himself will manifestly intervene in the affairs of man.

21-22. The ultimate objective of the Lord is the spiritual restoration of Israel to Himself. The return to the land is only an important precursor/prelude to that event. (See Jer. 33:7-8 Ezek. 36:24-28.)

23. Gentile believers owe a tremendous debt to the Jewish people. God will withhold from them His full blessing until they acknowledge their debt and seek to make amends by fulfilling their scriptural obligations.

(For more information on the subject of Israel, see Derek Prince's book, *The Last Word on the Middle East.*)

STUDY NO. 18
MESSIAH'S KINGDOM ESTABLISHED ON EARTH
Introduction:

Messiah's kingdom on earth will be ushered in by His judgments on all who have rejected God's mercy and opposed God's purposes in the preceding period. On the other hand, all believers who have been either resurrected or supernaturally changed at Messiah's coming will be allotted various positions of authority in His kingdom. With Jerusalem as His capital, Messiah will reign over all nations for 1,000 years bringing justice, peace, prosperity and the knowledge of God to the whole earth. Finally, He will offer up Himself and His kingdom in submission to God the Father.

Memory Work: 2 Tim. 2:11-12   Please check when memory card prepared ☐
(Review daily Luke 21:28)

A. JUDGMENTS THAT USHER IN MESSIAH'S KINGDOM

1. The coming of Messiah from heaven is described in 2 Thess. 1:6-10.

   (1) How will He deal with the wicked and disobedient? (v. 8)

   (2) What will be their punishment? (v. 9)

2. What will happen to the beast (antichrist) and the false prophet? (Rev. 19:20)

3. How will Messiah rule the nations on earth? (Rev. 19:11-15 Ps. 2:7-9)

4. When Messiah sets up His throne on earth, who will be gathered before Him for judgment? (Matt. 25:31-32 Joel 3:1-2)

5. These nations will be judged by the way they have treated a certain class of people. How does Jesus describe this class?
   (1) (Matt. 25:40)
   (2) (Joel 3:2)

6. What will be the double reward of those nations who have done what Messiah required?
   (1) (Matt. 25:34)
   (2) (Matt. 25:46)

7. What will be the punishment of those nations who have not done what Messiah required? (Matt. 25:41, 46)

B. THE POSITION OF RESURRECTED BELIEVERS

8. If we endure suffering for Messiah, what two rewards can we expect?
   (1) (Rom. 8:17)
   (2) (2 Tim. 2:12)

9. What position did Jesus promise to the apostles who had continued faithfully with Him? (Matt. 19:27-28)

10. To what kind of believer will Jesus give authority to rule the nations with Him? (Rev. 2:26-27)

11. What will be the double reward of those believers beheaded by the antichrist for their witness to Jesus? (Rev. 20:4-5)
    (1)
    (2)

12. Jesus told a parable about servants administering money committed to them by their master (Luke 19:12-26). What was the reward
    (1) Of the servant who achieved a tenfold increase? (Luke 19:16-17)

    (2) Of the servant who achieved a fivefold increase? (Luke 19:18-19)

13. Name two areas over which resurrected believers will rule as judges in the next age?
(1) (1 Cor. 6:2).. (2) (1 Cor. 6:3)..

C. A PROPHETIC PREVIEW OF MESSIAH'S KINGDOM

14. With what kind of scepter does Messiah rule? (Ps. 45:6   Heb 1:8)

....

15. Why has God anointed Messiah above all others? (Ps. 45:7   Heb. 1:9)

....

16. In what place has the Lord chosen to dwell forever? (Ps. 132:13-14)

....

17. What two names are given to the place in which the Lord will reign as king? (Is. 24:23)
(1) (Ps. 48:1-2).. (2) (Matt. 5:34-35)..

18. In the latter days what mountain will be raised above the surrounding mountains?
(Is. 2:2   Mic. 4:1)

....

19. Who will stream to this mountain? (Is. 2:2   Mic. 4:1)

....

20. What will God teach these nations? (Is. 2:3   Mic. 4:2)

....

21. What two things will go forth out of Zion and Jerusalem? (Is. 2:3   Mic. 4:2)
(1).. (2)..

22. When Messiah judges the nations, what two things will they no longer do? (Is. 2:4
Mic. 4:3)
(1)..
(2)..

23. For what special feast will nations go up to Jerusalem each year? (Zech. 14:16)

....

24. Psalm 72 foreshows various features of the reign of David's Son, the Messiah. For example:
(1) How will Messiah rule the poor? (vv. 2, 4)

....

(2) What three kinds of people will Messiah deliver? (v. 12)
(a).. (b).. (c)..
(3) What kind of person will flourish during Messiah's reign? (v. 7)

....

(4) Of what will there be abundance? (v. 7)

....

(5) What two things will all nations do to Messiah?
(a) (v. 11).. (b) (v. 17)..
25. What will be three permanent results of Messiah's righteous rule? (Is. 32:17)
(1).. (2).. (3)..
26. For how long will this period of Messiah's reign last? (Rev. 20:4-5)

....

27. What will Messiah do at the end of this period? (1 Cor. 15:24, 28)

....

28. What is the end purpose of God in all this? (1 Cor. 15:28)

....

Memory Work: 2 Timothy 2:11-12
Write out these verses from memory.

....

....

....

....

....

DO NOT TURN THIS PAGE UNTIL YOU HAVE COMPLETED ALL ANSWERS IN THIS STUDY

CORRECT ANSWERS AND MARKS

Question No.	Answers	Marks
1.	(1) He will take vengeance on them with flaming fire	1
	(2) Everlasting destruction from the presence of the Lord and from the glory of His power	2
2.	They will be cast alive into the lake of fire burning with brimstone	1
3.	With a rod of iron	1
4.	All nations	1
5.	(1) My brethren	1
	(2) My people, My heritage Israel	2
6.	(1) They will inherit Messiah's kingdom	1
	(2) They will receive eternal life	1
7.	Everlasting punishment in eternal fire prepared for the devil and his angels	2
8.	(1) We shall be glorified together with Him	1
	(2) We shall reign with Him	1
9.	To sit on twelve thrones judging the twelve tribes of Israel	2
10.	The one who overcomes and keeps Messiah's works until the end	2
11.	(1) To have part in the first resurrection	1
	(2) To reign with Christ for 1,000 years	1
12.	(1) Authority over ten cities	1
	(2) Authority over five cities	1
13.	(1) The world (2) Angels	2
14.	A scepter of righteousness	1
15.	Because He loves righteousness and hates wickedness	2
16.	Zion	1
17.	(1) Zion (2) Jerusalem	2
18.	The mountain of the Lord's house	1
19.	All nations	1
20.	His ways	1
21.	(1) The law (2) The word of the Lord	2
22.	(1) Lift up their swords against other nations	1
	(2) Learn war	1
23.	The Feast of Tabernacles	1
24.	(1) With justice	1
	(2) (a) The needy (b) The poor (c) The one who has no helper	3
	(3) The righteous	1
	(4) Peace	1
	(5) (a) Serve Him (b) Call Him blessed	2
25.	(1) Peace (2) Quietness (3) Assurance	3
26.	1,000 years	1
27.	Deliver the kingdom to God the Father and be subject to Him	2
28.	That God may be all in all	1

Consult Bible for written Memory Work

If word perfect, 4 marks for each verse 8
(1 mark off for each mistake. If more than three mistakes
in either verse, no marks for that verse.)   TOTAL 62

60% – 37   75% – 46   90% – 56

STUDY NO. 18: MESSIAH'S KINGDOM ESTABLISHED ON EARTH
NOTES ON CORRECT ANSWERS

(The numbers in the lefthand margin correspond to the
numbers of the correct answers on the previous page.)

1. Second Thess. 1:6-10 depicts the glory and power of Messiah's coming. All His enemies will be eternally banished, but His glory will be seen both in the angels who accompany Him and in the believers who will be caught up to meet Him. (Compare 1 Thess. 4:16-17.)

2. Rev. 13 reveals that, as this age draws to a close, human wickedness will come to a head in the person of a supremely wicked, but powerful, ruler described as "the (wild) beast." He is also called "the man of sin (lawlessness)," "the son of perdition" (2 Thess. 2:3), "the Antichrist" (1 John 2:18). He will be supported by an evil religious leader called "the false prophet." Together, they will seek to destroy all the followers of Jesus. (Compare Dan. 8:23-25.)

3. Rev. 19:11-15 depicts the coming of Jesus as King and Judge, with supreme power and authority to deal with all wickedness.

4-7. The judgment of the nations here described will determine which nations will be admitted to Messiah's kingdom and which will be excluded from it. The basis of their judgment will be the way they have treated the brothers of Jesus, the Jewish people. Jesus reckons anything done to the Jews – either good or bad – as done to Himself.

8-13. When Jesus returns and sets up His kingdom, all believers who have served Him faithfully in this life will be exalted to positions of honor and authority and will share with Jesus in the government of the universe. (Compare Rev. 3:21.) The degree of honor and authority assigned to believers will correspond to their faithfulness in serving Jesus in this age.

14-15. The distinctive feature of Messiah's character will be reflected in His kingdom: *righteousness*. Without righteousness there can never be true or lasting peace. (Compare Rom. 14:17.)

16-17. Messiah's kingdom will have its earthly capital in Jerusalem, or Zion. This is one important reason to pray for the peace of Jerusalem (Ps. 122:6). The rest of the earth will never know true peace until Jerusalem is established in peace.

18. At present, Mount Zion is lower than the mountains around it, but at Messiah's coming tremendous geologic changes will elevate Mount Zion above these surrounding mountains. (Compare Zech. 14:3-11.)

19-23. Jerusalem will then be the world center for worship, for government and for instruction in the ways of God. This will bring about worldwide disarmament and lasting peace.

24-25. The following are main features of Messiah's reign: righteousness; justice (especially for the underprivileged); peace; prosperity; universal acknowledgment of Messiah as God's appointed ruler. The establishment of His kingdom is the only realistic solution to the problems of disease, famine, injustice and war.

26. The precise duration of Messiah's reign is stated *six times* in Revelation 20 – in verses 2, 3, 4, 5, 6 and 7.

27-28. The delivering up of the kingdom to God the Father fulfills the principle stated in Rom. 11:36. All things have their source in God the Father and all things find their fulfillment in Him. However, the Father relates to the universe through His Son, the Messiah.

FINAL PROGRESS ASSESSMENT

Your faith and perseverance have been rewarded! You have now completed ALL THE MAIN 18 STUDIES. The only one remaining is an exercise in Personal Application.

It is time to pause and look back, to see how far you have come.

You have traced the Master Plan of history from its modest beginning in Abraham through the prophets and statesmen of Israel to the manifestation of the promised Messiah-Redeemer.

You have seen how Messiah's atonement provided the divine remedy for the two basic problems of the human race: sin and sickness. You have learned how to apply this remedy in your own life and in the lives of others.

You have seen how God's Word and God's Spirit, working together, can equip you with all you need for a life of fruitfulness and victory in the service of Messiah.

In studies 13, 14 and 15 you have learned: the importance and significance of water baptism; your responsibility to take your place in the long and honorable line of God's witnesses through the centuries; and the abundant provision that God has made for your material needs.

Finally, you have had a brief but exciting preview of the event with which this age will close: the personal return of Messiah in power and glory to establish His kingdom on earth.

In doing all this, you have searched out for yourself in the Bible the answers to more than *700 specific questions.*

You have also committed to memory *27 key verses of Scripture.*

There now awaits you the challenge of Study No. 19: Personal Application. But before moving on to that, be sure to work carefully through the Final Review on the opposite page.

FINAL REVIEW

Before you go on to Study No. 19, it is important for you to make sure that you have fully mastered all the material contained in studies 13 through 18. This will help you to prepare for the final Personal Application.

The method followed in the Final Review is similar to that followed in the first two.

First, read carefully through all the questions of the preceding six studies, together with the corresponding correct answers. Check that you now know and understand the correct answer to each question.

Second, review all the passages in these six studies which you have learned for Memory Work.

Third, read carefully through the following questions and consider how you would answer them. Each question is related in some way to the material you have been studying.

> 1. In what ways is Israel passing through the Red Sea a pattern for those who follow Messiah in baptism?

> 2. What are the main ways in which a believer should carry out his responsibility as a witness of the Messiah?

> 3. Describe briefly the sort of person concerning whom God promises: "Whatever he does shall prosper."

> 4. What are the main things we should do to prepare ourselves for Messiah's return?

Finally, write out on a separate sheet of paper your own answer to any *one* of the above questions.

* * * * *

There are no marks allotted for this Final Review. Its purpose is to help you *consolidate* all that you have been discovering. When you are satisfied that this has been achieved, turn the page to the final Study No. 19: Personal Application.

STUDY NO. 19

PERSONAL APPLICATION

Introduction:

In working through the previous eighteen studies, you have learned many important and life-changing truths from God's Word. But you must remember that knowledge, by itself, is never sufficient. The Bible never presents mere truth in the abstract. It always challenges us to apply the truth it teaches in a practical way to every area of our lives. Jesus put this very bluntly to His disciples: "If you know these things, happy are you if you do them" (John 13:17). It is not what we *know* that makes us happy, but only what we know *and do*.

The purpose of this final study is to help you assess both how much you have learned and how well you have been applying it.

Final Memory Work: James 1:25   Please check when memory card prepared ☐
(Review daily 2 Tim. 2:11-12)

SECTION A: Write below, in the spaces provided, four important truths from the Bible which you have learned from this course. In each case, write down the references to the passages in the Bible where that truth is found.

First truth...
....
....
....

Bible references...
....

Second truth...
....
....
....

Bible references...
....

Third truth...
....
....
....

Bible references...
....

Fourth truth...
....
....
....

Bible references...
....

SECTION B: On a separate sheet of paper, describe any important changes which have taken place in your life as a result of working through this course. Do you see any other areas of your life where there is a need for change: If so, what steps will you take to make the needed changes?

NOTE: There are no marks allotted for Sections A and B above.

Final Memory Work: James 1:25
Write out this verse from memory.

....

....

....

Consult Bible for written Memory Work

If word perfect, 4 marks... 4
(1 mark off for each mistake. If more
than 3 mistakes, no marks)   TOTAL 4

MARKS FOR THE COURSE

How to assess your own results:

Write your marks for each study in the space provided below in the right-hand column. Add up your own total and compare it with the standards given for Fair, Good or Excellent.

STUDY NO. 1	54	_____
STUDY NO. 2	49	_____
STUDY NO. 3	51	_____
STUDY NO. 4	61	_____
STUDY NO. 5	33	_____
STUDY NO. 6	80	_____
STUDY NO. 7	43	_____
STUDY NO. 8	46	_____
STUDY NO. 9	38	_____
STUDY NO. 10	46	_____
STUDY NO. 11	45	_____
STUDY NO. 12	61	_____
STUDY NO. 13	30	_____
STUDY NO. 14	40	_____
STUDY NO. 15	46	_____
STUDY NO. 16	49	_____
STUDY NO. 17	33	_____
STUDY NO. 18	62	_____
STUDY NO. 19	4	_____
TOTAL	**871**	**TOTAL** _____

FAIR	60% and over	523 – 652
GOOD	75% and over	653 – 783
EXCELLENT	90% and over	784 – 871

OTHER BOOKS BY DEREK PRINCE

Biography:
Appointment in Jerusalem

Guides to the Life of Faith:
Faith to Live By
How to Fast Successfully
Shaping History through Prayer and Fasting
The Grace of Yielding
The Marriage Covenant
Chords from David's Harp
God Is A Matchmaker

Systematic Bible Exposition:
The Last Word of the Middle East
Foundation Series (3 Volumes)
Christian Foundation Correspondence Course

For complete free catalog of books, audio cassettes, video cassettes, and other material by Derek Prince, write to:

Derek Prince Ministries – International
P.O. Box 300
Fort Lauderdale, Florida 33302
U.S.A.

or

Derek Prince Ministries – U.K.
P.O. Box 169
Enfield, Middlesex EN3 6PL
England